PECTS OF LEARNING

eacher Induction

Reinhartz, Editor

D1114624

tional Education Association Publication

CONTENTS

1. THE TEACHER INDUCTION PROCESS: PRESERVING THE OLD AND WELCOMING THE NEW: AN INTRODUCTION

by Judy Reinhartz

Teacher induction can be considered the mortar that cements preservice training to continued in-service professional development. In its simplest form, teacher induction is the process of welcoming and helping beginners adjust to their new roles as in-service teachers. Because as Cruickshank and Callahan (1983) noted, the distance in linear feet may be short from the teacher's desk to the students, yet "... it is probably the largest psychological distance that these young adults have traveled in such a brief time" (pp. 251–52). The gradual introduction of new teachers into the teaching profession may seem quite normal and certainly within the natural scheme of things, with experienced teachers assuming a key role in this process.

At least in the United States, as it turns out, the process of gradually inducting new members into the teaching profession in any systematic way is more the exception than the rule. At best, some schools have an informal buddy system, with a buddy functioning more as a friend than mentor to the beginning teacher. Consequently, a buddy does not have specific roles to play or responsibilities to facilitate the helping process for beginning teachers (Shulman and Colbert 1987).

In fact, the teaching profession is one of the very few, if not the only profession, in which beginners are expected to assume full responsibilities the first day on the job (Huling-Austin 1988). In addition, beginning teachers often are assigned multiple preparations, lower-ability students, and no permanent classroom (*Beginning Teacher Induction Plan for Texas Schools* 1988). In effect we give the "... hardest job to the least experienced ..." (*ASCD Update* 1987, p. 6).

The literature supports this situation and a more systematic plan needs to be developed to ease the newcomer into the teaching profession. The research base is not only present, but it provides direction for developing and implementing teacher induction programs. The plan selected by individual school systems should be based on local needs. Without such a plan, beginning teachers may become discouraged and leave teaching; the dropout rate for new teachers will continue to escalate to proportions that could rival the number of students who drop out. As teacher surpluses turn to teacher shortages, teacher retention will become more important in the future. Schlechty and Vance (1983) estimate that at the national level, 30 percent of the teachers will leave during their first or second year of teaching and 50 percent will leave after four years. The supply of new teachers is projected to run one-third behind demand by 1992 (*ASCD Update* 1987, p. 6). The situation is compounded when recruiting and retaining minority teachers.

The case has been made time and time again that it is unrealistic and unfair to expect new teachers to function as proficiently and successfully as veterans. Secondly, it appears clear that in-service teachers should be regarded as experienced members of the profession who provide ongoing support and assistance to newcomers and should regard newcomers as underdeveloped talents. As new members of the teaching profession, beginning teachers need help in developing "coping" strategies, strategies that will lead to effective teaching. "These coping strategies can then 'crystallize' into a teaching style that is utilized throughout the teacher's career" (Huling-Austin 1988, p. 1). In effect, new teachers are "...trying to make sense out of a world they thought they understood" (Rieger and Zimpher 1989, p. 2).

Effective teaching and delivering quality instruction are lifelong goals and an integral part of teacher professional development. Newcomers have tremendous potential and should be guided and encouraged to grow and develop. They need formal, helpful supervision that is formative and not summative in nature (Beach and Reinhartz 1989). Attention needs to be focused on who is hired, their teaching assignment, and the type and quality of the teacher induction program established (Rand Corporation 1987). In an induction school, newcomers work side by side with experienced colleagues who can help them meet the many challenges waiting for them in elementary as well as secondary classrooms across the nation.

Teacher induction programs need to integrate new practices with those found to be tried and true. These practices will help in-service teachers and newcomers alike to meet the changing nature of tomorrow's schools. The process of teacher induction, then, should be viewed as ongoing, comprehensive, necessary, and a way of revitalizing our profession. It is in our own best interest that experienced teachers should not only endorse teacher induction but become leaders in the design and implementation of programs that meet the needs of faculty and students at the local level. With such an approach, the tried and true methods of teaching will be practiced along with newly developed ones. For without both, the teaching profession may be in jeopardy and the students and society will be the losers. As Mary Hatwood Futrell, President of the National Education Association, remarked after the Rand Corporation released the report, *Effective Teacher Selection*, "You cannot ignore the student populations; to do so may extinguish the American Dream."

Brooks (1987) is optimistic about teacher induction when he says that it "...holds promise as good medicine for the profession..." (p. 1). Teacher induction is gaining acceptance as more and more school systems find it a positive force in preserving the highly prized practices that experienced teachers use and in introducing newer innovative practices found in the teaching repertoires of beginning teachers.

This book is intended for a wide audience, with particular attention focused on administrators and policymakers, teacher educators, and beginning and experienced teachers. For the administrators and policymakers responsible for making decisions about retention and continued professional development, the book provides an overview of the various forms of teacher induction programs, the current knowledge base, and what is occurring nationally. This information may prove helpful to those who are being given more responsibility for initiating teacher induction at the state or local level.

It is our hope that teacher educators will use this book as the link between what is known about preparing teachers and in-servicing new teachers. Teacher educators are in a key position to forge a smooth transition between what is taught to those planning to teach and what they can expect as first-year teachers. Furthermore, information regarding induction may help to establish a closer working relationship between supervising teachers and their roles and responsibilities as mentors to beginning teachers. In addition, the book may prove helpful to individual beginning and veteran teachers in stimulating their thinking about and reflecting on the complexities of their roles as teachers and instructional leaders.

This volume offers vital and timely information about the teacher induction process and its different components. The following five chapters provide a backdrop to the topic, with particular attention given to what the literature says about the teacher induction process and the research that has been conducted to contribute to the existing knowledge base. A great deal has been written on this topic, particularly during the late 1970s and 1980s. Most of what has been written focuses on the instructional concerns of beginning teachers, with the newer studies concentrating on the situational/contextual building concerns, the role of the principal, and personal concerns. The latter areas may be the focus for additional research and provide the needed direction to teacher induction in the next decade.

The final three chapters include descriptions of several successful programs that are now in existence. Some of these programs have been operating for some time, while others are relative newcomers. For teacher induction programs to be judged successful, it is essential that models be developed that help prospective users to determine why the program is successful and what conditions are needed to effectively replicate it in a different location with different administrators, faculty, and staff.

In this volume, Leslie Huling-Austin reviews the current literature since 1977; she provides a comprehensive picture of the different types of investigations that have been included under the ruberic of teacher induction. Huling-Austin has spent time carefully studying different types of induction programs described in the literature and has become one of the foremost authorities on the subject. After identifying the 17 studies reviewed, she grouped them around five commonly accepted goals: (a) to improve teaching performance; (b) to increase the retention of promising beginning teachers during the induction years; (c) to promote the personal and professional well-being of beginning teachers; (d) to satisfy mandated requirements related to induction and certification; and (e) to transmit the culture of the system to beginning teachers. These goals served as the organizational framework for analyzing them. According to Huling-Austin, teacher induction programs can be successful only if and when the activities of the program are carefully selected and targeted toward specific goals.

James D. Greenberg and Maurice C. Erly focus on the larger picture of teacher induction, namely the context variables or what makes a building supportive for new teachers. Their chapter contains a description of a research project conducted by the authors that gathered data regarding the perceptions of new teachers and the environment of the school. A questionnaire was administered to 368 new teachers hired at the beginning of the 1986–1987 school year. Teachers responded to questions in the following areas: demographics, teacher concerns, and extra duties performed. The instrument included a self-report section in which the teachers were to include three things they found helpful at the building level, three things they did not, and three things they would like to see done, but weren't. Greenberg and Erly are encouraged by the findings from the study, but recommend that the data be given "finer cuts." They believe more attention needs to be given to administrative decisions made at the building level regarding teaching assignments, instructional and noninstructional responsibilities, individual classes, etc., assigned to beginning teachers.

Sandra J. Odell describes a research study conducted at a major university using interview data. This approach was used to determine the motivation, attitudes, expectations, and concerns of beginning elementary teachers and to determine the degree of change in teacher practices during the first year of teaching. The 18 teachers who participated in the study were drawn from a population of 180 first-year elementary teachers. Nine clinical support teachers were selected to work with the 18 beginning elementary teachers. The interview approach was used to collect the data. The interview, which was taped, consisted of seven open-ended questions and the results reported as percentages were encouraging. The majority of the new teachers felt motivated about teaching and, more importantly, they would make the same choice again, if given the chance. Odell attributes these positive attitudes to the "friendly critics" who provided support throughout the school year.

The results of this research effort seemed to be consistent with those generated by a previous study conducted by Odell, Laughlin, and Ferrara (1987) using direct observational approaches, with one exception. The one exception was the degree of help requested by first-year teachers from clinical support teachers. As Odell concludes that although the data generated in the current study do not reveal that the characteristics of beginning teachers in the induction program directly differ from those not receiving induction support, it would appear that teachers in her study are more motivated to teach and more focused on instruction than most other first-year teachers.

Louise Bay Waters and Victoria L. Bernhardt provide a detailed account of the many varied roles and responsibilities of support teachers. Often support teachers perform tasks that are formative in nature—advisor, confident, observer, and helper. Table 1 is an excellent visual that clearly identifies the roles, focus of the responsibilities, and the characteristics sought after in the support teacher. Helping experienced teachers take a lead in the induction process should be applauded, but a teacher does not automatically become a "support teacher." It takes work and some skills learned and practiced in a cooperative setting. Not all teachers want or should serve as mentors to beginning teachers. But those who do, need help in developing supervisory skills and abilities to provide psychological and technical support as well. It should be a learning experience for both the veteran as well as the new teacher. Both should benefit and Waters and Bernhardt provide the veteran teacher with food for thought and put in perspective how important experience is in the induction process.

8

Carol P. Etheridge provides real-life scenarios of beginning teachers; these case studies can be helpful for newcomers and veteran teachers alike. In addition, they serve as a valuable source of information about the triumphs, disappointments, concerns, and problems of beginning teachers as they enter the profession. The voices of "real" teachers are often overlooked, yet information in this form offers practical knowledge that only those involved in the situation can provide. Because practitioner analyses remain relatively small (Shulman and Colbert 1987), the collection of case studies included here is valuable as it adds this type of knowledge to a growing body of literature. These narrative accounts provide an understanding about teaching that only can be gained through practitioner experience. These case studies, in some instances provide a lesson, illustrate a principle, and/or offer thoughts and feelings about an experience, situation, or incident. As the case studies are read, recurring themes become evident that can guide a discussion and actions, and even suggest possible direction for practice in the future.

Marvin A. Henry provides an example of a successful teacher induction program for first-year teachers. He begins with an explanation of three types of teacher support: mentor, peer, and university support. For Henry, mentor support, peer support, and support from teacher preparation programs are key to a teacher induction program. He agrees with Pigge and Marso that the supervisory triad, which has served student teaching so successfully, should be put in place at the in-service phase for first-year teachers.

Henry then provides a detailed account of the CREDIT program (Certification, Renewal Experiences Designed to Improve Teaching) at Indiana State University, which uses a multiple support system. Twenty new teachers in 15 schools have been a part of the CREDIT program, and based on data collected and analyzed from questionnaires, the program has proved to be very helpful for them. In the evaluation procedures, a control group was used to determine whether there were changes in teacher perceptions about teaching and to determine whether the project objectives were met. When compared to the control group, the CREDIT interns demonstrated significant changes in the areas of mastery learning, motivation, use of higher-order questioning, and other measured teacher skills. Additionally, the CREDIT interns indicated a desire to stay in teaching, and as indicated in a follow-up study, remained for a second year. These are significant results in light of the 26.5 percent dropout rate for teachers in Indiana during the first two years of teaching. Henry attributes the success of CREDIT to the multiple support system.

Before describing the teacher induction for first-year teachers at the

University of Wisconsin–Whitewater, Leonard J. Varah, Warren S. Theune, and Linda Parker set the stage by providing a brief, but thorough review of the literature on the subject. Program designers will find their description of the teacher induction program extremely helpful not only because of the details included (goals, mentor teacher responsibilities, orientation objectives, financial arrangements), but also because of its detailed account of the research design used. Although the sample reported was relatively small, the data presented, using interviews and questionnaires, suggest that the teacher induction at the University of Wisconsin–Whitewater is meeting its primary objective, namely enhancement of teacher growth.

In the final chapter, Alvah M. Kilgore and Julie A. Kozisek present a detailed description of a teacher support/induction program for beginning teachers from a higher education perspective. They explored the role of the college or university in the induction process. The induction program described involved Teachers College of the University of Nebraska, Concordia Teachers College, and Doane College, which were part of a state Consortium. Students came from all three institutions and participated in a variety of experiences and were provided with various services during their first year of teaching.

Kilgore and Kozisek conclude that the data between groups were not significantly different in several areas, but their findings are worthy of consideration for a variety of reasons. First, the data generated by self-reporting measures, on-site observations of beginning teachers, and participation in regional seminars build a rather convincing case of the "tenuous life of first-year teachers," even when help is provided by colleges/universities. Second, the findings confirm and support previous research on the tremendous influence the school environment has on socializing the first-year teacher. Last, the role that college personnel can play may be more peripheral in nature (offering feedback, intervening to ease the transition, serving as facilitator) rather than direct. Therefore, the type of support that colleges/universities can provide certainly needs to consider the more powerful context, school variables. The list of concerns of first-year teachers can also be helpful to designers of induction programs because they serve to remind us of the "reality shock" first-year teachers experience.

In the Appendix, John M. Johnston reviews over 40 articles, books, and other references. Only two of the articles were written in 1969 and 1979, respectively; others were written during the 1980s. It is an excellent collection of materials and the annotations are descriptive and detailed enough to provide a comprehensive picture of the program or methodology under discussion. The Annotated Bibliography provides a synthesis of the knowledge that is now a part of the teacher induction literature.

CONCLUSION

It is evident from the discussions that follow that local school systems within several states are moving slowly to formalize and implement the teacher induction process. For example, in 1986, 17 states had a pilot program in place and 14 more were in the planning stages; yet 20 others reported no action (Huling-Austin 1988). The major problem, according to Hawk and Robards (1987), is funding. Therefore, steps need to be taken at the local level where the concern and nurturing instinct are at their greatest.

Now that we know what researchers have said and we have a general idea about successful teacher induction programs, the question is, where do we go from here? The answer lies with each of us as teachers and our voices needed to be heard. Teachers need to be the leaders in shaping and implementing teacher induction programs that will ensure for generations to come a way of preserving our heritage and teaching practices as a profession.

REFERENCES

ASCD Update. 1987. Study backs induction schools to help new teachers stay teachers. Washington, DC: Association of Supervision and Curriculum Development.

Beach, D. M., and Reinhartz, J. 1989. *Supervision: Focus on instruction.* New York: Harper & Row.

Beginning Teacher Induction Plan for Texas Schools. 1988, November 8. Draft.

Brooks, D., ed. 1987. *Teacher induction: A new beginning.* Reston, VA: Association of Teacher Educators.

Cruickshank, D. R., and Callahan, R. 1983. The other side of the desk: Stages and problems of teacher development. *The Elementary School Journal* 83: 250–58.

Hawk, P. P., and Robards, S. 1987. Statewide teacher induction programs. In *Teacher induction—A new beginning*, ed. D. Brooks. Reston, VA: Association of Teacher Educators.

Huling-Austin, L. 1988, March. *Teacher induction, Texas directors of field experiences*. Paper presented at the Spring Conference on Teacher Education, El Paso, TX.

Rand Corporation. 1987. *Effective Teacher Selection*. Santa Monica, CA. Report Code R–3467–NIE–CSTP.

Reiger, S. R., and simpher, N. L. 1989, February. *From inductee to mentor to leader: Reflections on the professional development of teachers*. Paper presented at the annual meeting of the Association of Teacher Educators, St. Louis, MO.

Schlechty, P., and Vance, V. 1983. Recruitment selection, and retention: The shape of the teaching force. *The Elementary School Journal* 83: 469–87.

Shulman, J. H., and Colbert, J. A., eds. 1987, November. *The mentor teacher casebook*. Eugene, OR: ERIC Clearinghouse on Educational Management and San Francisco: Far West Laboratory for Educational Research and Development.

2. A SYNTHESIS OF RESEARCH ON TEACHER INDUCTION PROGRAMS AND PRACTICES*

by Leslie Huling-Austin

INTRODUCTION AND METHODOLOGY

Author's Point of View

The motivation for this [chapter] is more pragmatic than scholarly. In my dealings with school practitioners, policymakers and researchers across the country, I am encountering with increasing frequency the question of what the research base "says" about teacher induction. Those asking primarily want to know if there are research data that support the assumption that teacher induction programs make a difference, and if there are research findings that indicate certain induction practices or program components are likely to have positive effects.

In order to address these questions, I have attempted to synthesize research on teacher induction programs and practices. I established three criteria on which to select studies for inclusion in my synthesis. In order to be included, studies must have been:

1. data-based (i.e., data must have been systematically collected and analyzed)

2. focused on beginning teachers in an induction program (i.e., teachers must have been receiving some type of formal induction assistance; studies of beginning teachers not in an induction program were not included), and

3. reported since 1977.

A number of sources were used to identify studies for inclusion in this synthesis including: an extensive search of the ERIC database, three ERIC Digests (1986) on related topics, a survey of members of a national teacher induction network, programs of the annual meetings of the

---

*This chapter is reprinted with permission from *Centering Teacher Education*, Fall 1988, pp. 19–28. Copyright 1988, Centering Teacher Education, University of Texas–Arlington.

American Educational Research Association (AERA) for the past five years, a monograph on teacher induction (Brooks 1987), published proceedings from three conferences with a focus on teacher induction (Griffin and Hukill 1983; Huling-Austin, Putman, Edwards, and Galvez-Hjornevik 1985; Hord, O'Neal, and Smith 1985), and several major journals devoting theme issues to the topic of teacher induction (*Educational Leadership*, November, 1985; *Journal of Teacher Education*, January–February, 1986; *Kappa Delta Pi Record*, July–August, 1986; and *Action in Teacher Education*, Winter 1987). These sources yielded more than 25 studies that appeared to meet the three criteria outlined above. After a careful analysis of each study, a number of studies were excluded for various reasons (see "Selection of Studies" on pp. 16–17) and the list was trimmed to 17 studies which ultimately were deemed appropriate for inclusion in the synthesis. The titles and authors of these 17 studies appear in Figure 1.

I feel compelled to mention that from my viewpoint of one who has spent considerable time studying the teacher induction literature, the list of studies at first glance is somewhat surprising. Some of the studies included will be unknown to most who stay current on teacher induction literature as the studies have not yet appeared in professional publications. Conversely, many "key" induction references are not included in the list of studies synthesized primarily because the authors were either not reporting research or their studies were conducted on beginning teachers who were not participating in induction programs. I would like to emphasize that in my opinion many pieces of work not included in this synthesis are extremely informative and useful to the field of teacher induction; I recommend "Teacher Induction: A New Beginning" (Brooks 1987) and "The Knowledge Base for Teacher Induction: A Selected Annotated Bibliography" (Johnston 1988).

Finally, I believe it is important to point out that I am viewing this [chapter] not as a finished product but rather as a modest beginning. I certainly intend to expand and revise this description of a "research base" for teacher induction as additional studies become available and I welcome others to take this as a first step and to build upon it.

Organizational Framework

A number of organizational frameworks were considered for this synthesis. Because the 17 studies vary greatly in terms of their rigor, size, and comprehensiveness, serious consideration was given to grouping studies according to their various characteristics and then comparing and contrasting their findings accordingly. Another approach that was consid-

Figure 1
17 Studies Included in Synthesis

Blackburn (1977)	The First-Year Teacher: Perceived Needs, Intervention Strategies and Results
Brooks (1986)	Richardson New Teacher Induction Program: Final Data Analysis and Report
Butler (1987)	Lessons Learned About Mentoring in Two Fifth-Year Teacher Preparation-Induction Programs
Eisner (1984)	First Year Evaluation Results from Oklahoma's Entry-Year Assistance Committees
Friske and Combs (1986)	Teacher Induction Programs: An Oklahoma Perspective
Grant and Zeichner (1981)	Inservice Support for First Year Teachers: The State of the Scene
Hegler and Dudley (1986)	Beginning Teacher Induction: A Progress Report
Hidalgo (1986-87)	The Evolving Concerns of First–Year Junior High school Teachers in Difficult Settings: Three Case Studies
Hoffman, Edwards, O'Neal, Barnes and Paulissen (1986)	A Study of State-Mandated Beginning Teacher Programs
Huffman and Leak (1986)	Beginning Teachers' Perceptions of Mentors
Huling-Austin and Murphy (1987)	Assessing the Impact of Teacher Induction Programs: Implications for Program Development
Huling-Austin, Putman and Galvez-Hjornevik (1985)	Model Teacher Induction Project Study Findings: Final Report
Kilgore and Kozisek (1988)	The Effects of a Planned Induction Program on First-Year Teachers: A Research Report
Marockie and Looney (1988)	Evaluating Teacher Induction in Ohio County Schools, Wheeling, West Virginia
Odell (1986)	Induction Support of New Teachers: A Functional Approach: A Functional Report
Summers (1987)	Summative Evaluation Report: project CREDIT
Wildman, Niles, Magliaro, McLaughlin and Drill (1987)	Virginia's Colleague Teachers Project: Focus on Beginning Teachers' Adaptation to Teaching

15

ered was to isolate induction practices being studied and to identify findings related to the various practices across studies. However, after much deliberation, both of these approaches were discarded because the author feared such frameworks would quickly become so fragmented that the resulting product would not be very helpful to practitioners and policymakers who are requesting that a research-base be identified in order to help them make decisions and design programs.

The framework finally selected for use in this synthesis is focused around commonly accepted goals of teacher induction programs. Huling-Austin (1986) identified four such goals that she believes are common to most induction programs: These goals include:

1. to improve teaching performance

2. to increase the retention of promising beginning teachers during the induction years

3. to promote the personal and professional well-being of beginning teachers

4. to satisfy mandated requirements related to induction and certification.

Since that publication, Huling-Austin (1988) has added a fifth goal to the list that she believes is prevalent among many programs, although probably to a lesser degree than the other four. This fifth goal is:

5. to transmit the culture of the system to beginning teachers.

In addition to categories devoted to each of the five goals above, a final category of the framework is devoted to other noteworthy findings that are either not clearly related to one of the five goals of teacher induction programs or cut across so many of the goals that it would be inappropriate to categorize them under a single goal. The use of this miscellaneous category provides for the inclusion of important findings without forcing them into categories in which they do not clearly fit.

SYNTHESIS OF SELECTED INDUCTION STUDIES

Selection of Studies

Even using the three previously explained criteria for study selection, determining which studies to include in this synthesis was not an easy task. In order for this synthesis to be meaningful, it was necessary to maintain a sharp focus on induction programs and practices and thus it was also necessary to make a number of arbitrary decisions to clarify what studies should and should not be included. Among the studies that were excluded were those which were predominantly follow-up studies of graduates from university teacher education programs (for example, Arends 1982; McCaleb 1984). Follow-up studies were excluded because some graduates were in settings with induction programs while others were not, and generally no attempt was made to organize or analyze data according to this distinction of supported induction vs. nonsupported. Studies that focused on the general phenomena of mentoring (not in conjunction with a formal induction program) were excluded (see Galvez-Hjornevik 1985) as well as studies that had as their primary focus the benefits of induction programs for experienced personnel as opposed to beginning teachers (for example, Hawk 1984). Studies that were primarily descriptions of programs and program components were also excluded (for example Elias, McDonald, Stevenson, Simon, and Fisher 1980). It should also be mentioned that when the same data were reported in several different sources, the author attempted to select the single most comprehensive source for inclusion in this synthesis.

Even by limiting the number of studies included, it was still necessary to select only representative findings from each study. No attempt was made to synthesize every finding of every study, rather the author attempted to identify the study's strongest contribution(s) and focus on these. Occasionally, a common point or finding was present in so many different studies that it was not feasible to reference them all. In this instance, the author chose to reference those studies that she believed most clearly made the point. In addition, every attempt was made not to misrepresent a study by highlighting insignificant findings or taking findings out of context. In order not to unnecessarily belabor the point of how studies and findings were selected for inclusion in this synthesis, let us proceed.

Goal 1: To Improve Teaching Performance

The idiosyncratic nature of teaching makes it difficult to measure teaching effectiveness or to compare the teaching performance of one group of teachers with any other group of teachers. Even so, facilitators of induction programs, like the profession at large, are beginning to tackle this issue and to attempt to document the effects of induction programs on teaching performance.

The only study identified that attempted to compare student achievement of first-year teachers in an induction program with first-year teachers not receiving induction support, found no significant differences in

17

the student achievement of control and experimental teachers (Blackburn 1977, p. 7). This study did, however, find significant differences in how principals rated the teaching competency of experimental and control teachers. The teaching competency of experimental teachers who had cooperating teachers assigned to them on a one-to-one basis were rated significantly higher than that of "nonsupported" first-year teachers.

Another controlled study was conducted by Project CREDIT (Certification Renewal Experiences Designed to Improve Teaching), a teacher induction program sponsored by Indiana State University and funded through the Indiana Teacher Quality Act (PL 102–1985). This study indicated that first-year teachers participating in the project showed specific and significant measurable changes when compared with the control group (Summers 1987). The evaluation report indicated:

> CREDIT interns demonstrated (1) a significant gain in the use of mastery learning and mastery learning theory, (2) increased motivation to understand and use higher order questions, (3) increased inclination to teach critical thinking skills, (4) increased awareness of state and local curriculum guides, (5) enhanced ability to communicate with parents, and (6) improved ability to communicate with the public at large. (pp. 33–34)

In an evaluation of the Oklahoma Entry-Year Assessment Program (Elsner 1984), committee members including entry-year teachers, teacher consultants, school administrators and higher education representatives were asked to rate the beginning teacher's knowledge, skills, and competencies in 10 areas at the beginning of the school year and again at the end. Data from this sample of more than 200 respondents indicated that first-year teachers made significant progress in planning skills, handling class discussions, preparation of unit and lesson plans, management of discipline problems, and the ability to teach or train others (p. 7).

In a study by Huling-Austin and Murphy (1987) in an end-of-year interview, first-year teachers were asked what changes they had made as a result of the assistance they had received through their induction programs. These changes were programs documented by the researchers in a full-page figure (p. 25) which displayed items such as "I've changed little things like voice inflection and eye contact," "I've changed my pacing; I was going too fast, especially through the transitions," and "To use different techniques like going from the chalkboard to the overhead in the same class." The researchers comment:

> It is interesting to note both the number and nature of the changes mentioned. The list indicates that a substantial amount of change is

attributed by first-year teachers to the assistance they received through the induction program. Also, most of the changes are of an instructional nature and are of the type that directly influence the quality of instruction with students. While it is difficult to quantify, based on the changes reported, it is reasonable to conclude that the teaching of the participating first-year teachers was improved as a result of their involvement in the induction programs. (pp. 23–26)

Using a similar approach for measuring improvement in teaching performance, Marockie and Looney (1988) measured beginning teachers' use of suggestions and recommendations acquired from their Teacher Induction Program (TIP). The 15 beginning teachers in their study listed 20 different ideas which they had used that had emanated from the TIP. Sixty-seven percent of the beginning teachers listed "use of time" as having impact on their instruction after presentation at a TIP seminar. Thirty-three percent listed "praise," "conducting class in a businesslike manner," "classroom management techniques," "use of space," and "recording-keeping." The researchers concluded:

These responses suggest that instruction was improved through the use of practices translated from current educational research presented at TIP seminars. Since research findings presented in the seminars were those that have stood the test of time in terms of statistical evidence and systematic inquiry, it may be conjectured that instruction may have improved in the new teachers' classrooms. (p. 6)

It is important to point out that as a profession we have a long way to go in being able to measure teaching performance with confidence. The problem is further compounded by the fact that it is unrealistic to use the same evaluation standards for beginning teachers that are used for experienced teachers. Teacher induction programs have only begun to address the issue of program influences on teaching performance. However, some progress has been made in this area and hopefully as improved evaluation measures, techniques, and instruments are developed specifically for use with beginning teachers, these will be incorporated into the overall evaluation designs of more induction programs.

Goal 2: To Increase the Retention of Promising Beginning Teachers During the Induction Years

It is well documented in the literature that without induction support and assistance many potentially good teachers become discouraged and abandon their teaching careers (Ryan, Newman, Mager, Applegate, Las-

19

ley, Flora, and Johnston 1980). Schlechty and Vance (1983) estimate that approximately 30 percent of beginning teachers leave the profession during their first two years, compared to the overall teacher turnover rate of 6 percent per year. The turnover rate of new teachers does not level out to the overall rate of 6 percent until the fifth or sixth year. Of all beginning teachers who enter the profession, 40 to 50 percent will leave during the first seven years of their career and in excess of two-thirds of those will do so in the first four years of teaching. These figures are especially depressing in light of evidence that suggests that those teachers who are the most academically talented leave in the greatest numbers (Schlechty and Vance 1983).

Just how much teacher induction programs have influenced the retention of beginning teachers is not well documented. However, of the evidence that is available, it appears that at least some induction programs are having the desired effects on retention of beginning teachers. For example, Project CREDIT conducted by Indiana State University reported that after one year of operation all 21 participating first-year teachers indicated a desire to return to teaching the following year. This compares to figures from a statewide needs assessment which indicated that 26.5 percent of Indiana teachers who entered teaching dropped out within two years and 62 percent had dropped out within five years (Summers 1987, p. 34).

Similarly impressive results have been reported by the University of Alabama/Birmingham First-Year Teacher Pilot Program (Blackburn 1977). In this effort, data were collected from 100 first-year teachers receiving induction support and 100 first-year teachers in a control group not receiving support. Of the 100 teachers in the experimental group, all but four taught the following year; 20 of the control teachers did not teach the second year (p. 9).

In the fall of 1983, Doane College in Nebraska instituted an induction program as one component of its teacher education program. In 1987, the program reported 24 of the 25 teachers participating in the induction program have remained in the teaching profession, some now in their fourth year of teaching (Hegler and Dudley 1986, p. 54). Again, while it is difficult to know exactly to what degree retention is influenced by induction support, with a 96 percent retention rate overall it is difficult to deny that the induction program is having some positive influence on retention.

It is somewhat ironic that while increased teacher retention is probably one of the greatest potential impacts of induction programs, this particular effect has probably been investigated less than any others. To date, very few programs have systematically collected and reported retention data and this clearly is an area in need of additional investigation. However, premature as it is to speculate, the data reported to date indicate that teacher induction programs potentially hold a great deal of promise for retaining greater numbers of beginning teachers in the profession and thus reducing the waste of resources and human potential associated with unnecessarily high teacher attrition during the beginning years.

Goal 3: To Promote the Personal and Professional Well-Being of Beginning Teachers

Not all beginning teachers experience personal and professional trauma during their first year even without the support of an induction program. However, many do and in extreme cases beginning teachers have been known to lose self-confidence, experience extreme stress and anxiety, and to question their own competence as a teacher and a person. For example, Hidalgo (1986–87), in studying emergency credentialed teachers in the Los Angeles Unified School District found that teachers had persistent personal and management preoccupations which "obstructed, and even paralyzed their progress toward more sophisticated use of teaching knowledge" (p. 78). In several studies he described in detail their anxieties, insecurities, and frustrations.

Huling-Austin (1986) contends that a profession has a responsibility for the well-being of its members as well as its clients, and that it is professionally irresponsible not to provide beginning teachers with personal support when it is needed. Teacher induction programs can serve as one avenue of providing this support, and many studies have reported positive outcomes in this area. One such example provided by Huffman and Leak (1986) is related to the "mentor" teacher component of the North Carolina Beginning Teacher Program. "Mentor teachers were found to have provided 'positive reinforcement,' 'guidance and moral support,' 'patience and understanding,' and even 'a shoulder to cry on'" (p. 23). Brooks (1986) in his work with the Richardson ISD (Texas) New Teacher Induction Program found that beginning teachers in the program reported increased feelings of competence, motivation, belonging, support, and attention as a result of their experiences in the program.

In their work with first-year teachers in the Virginia Beginning Teacher Assistance Program, researchers investigated the effects of the emotional support beginning teachers received from experienced teachers in the program (Wildman, Niles, Magliaro, McLaughlin, and Drill 1987). They noted:

21

The chance to interact with a colleague by asking questions, sharing materials or planning collaboratively has other benefits of an emotional nature. The beginning teachers sense this support from the helping or nurturing attitudes of their colleagues and depend on it to get them through those first, difficult, lonely months. The beginning teachers report being comforted [when] the experienced teachers share their trials and frailties with them. In addition, the recognition they receive from the experienced colleague that they are performing satisfactorily is important to the beginning teacher in developing their positive teaching self-concept. In the first several months of school a number of beginning teachers report that their experienced colleague is the only person who has commented on their teaching competence. This is particularly true in our high school pairs. Thus, even general feedback on performance during the early months by the experienced colleague reduces the uncertainty of the beginner that they are meeting expectations. This reduction of uncertainty in turn creates a feeling of security. (p. 12)

Huling-Austin and Murphy (1987) studied groups of beginning teachers across the country who were and were not participating in teacher induction programs. Using a questionnaire designed to measure the beginning teacher's perception of his/her own effectiveness and the desirability of the teaching profession, they found that, "Responses from sites that had no formal induction program in operation were noticeably less desirable than the other sites" (p. 33). Summers (1987) found a similar situation in Project CREDIT. Control group comparisons revealed that intern teachers completed the year with significantly healthier attitudes and perceptions about teaching than did a similar group of beginning teachers who did not have the CREDIT support program. Control group data revealed that nonsupported beginning teachers reported deteriorating attitudes or teaching perceptions in 88 or 98 surveyed variables (pp. 33–34). These findings from these two studies suggest that when beginning teachers are not supported they may begin to question their own effectiveness and their decisions to become teachers.

Interestingly, while beginning teachers often report that the emotional support they received was the most beneficial aspect of their teacher induction program, Odell (1986) found in analyzing categories of support provided to first-year teachers, that emotional support accounted for only a small percentage of the assistance provided. She wrote, "Although emotional support was of considerable importance across semesters, clinical support teachers generally offered more assistance with the formal teaching processes to new teachers than emotional support" (p. 28). This may suggest that emotional support is very important and without it beginning teachers have difficulty dealing with other matters. However, once emotional support is established, beginning teachers do not require large amounts of such support but rather can "move on" rather quickly to deal with instructional matters.

Goal 4: To Satisfy Mandated Requirements Related to Induction and Certification

Once a mandated program is implemented in a sense the mandate has been satisfied, but the more important question is to what degree the initial "intent" of the mandate is actually being addressed. There is some evidence that mandated state induction programs are "working." Blackburn (1977) in his report on the University of Alabama/Birmingham First-Year Teacher Pilot Program noted, "Despite some program shortcomings, the project demonstrated that the local school systems, the State Department of Education, and institutions of higher education can work together and that the cooperative effort can result in a positive difference in the behavior of teachers" (p. 12).

Elsner (1984) in his evaluation of the first year of the Oklahoma Entry-Year Assistance Program wrote:

> For a new program with no model to follow the Entry-Year Assistance Program achieved an unusual number of their stated objectives. It appears that much of the apprehension expressed by some school administrators prior to program implementation had disappeared and that higher education faculty members made a significant contribution to the success of the program. Lines of communication have developed between teacher educators and practitioners in the field. (p. 7)

Friske and Combs (1986) also worked with the Oklahoma Entry-Year Assistance Program and concluded that the program by-and-large has been implemented across the state. Their concern, however, is that studies on the program to date have focused on how the program has been implemented and the factors influencing implementation, but have not examined the extent to which the program has fulfilled the original intent of "improving the quality of teaching in Oklahoma."

A similar concern was expressed by another set of researchers in their study of two state-mandated teacher induction programs (Hoffman, Edwards, O'Neal, Barnes, and Paulissen 1986). They wrote:

> At the school level, our analyses of implementation focused on the work of the support teams with the beginning teacher. It is useful to

23

draw a distinction at this level between procedural compliance and substantive implementation of program requirements. Procedurally, the teams included in our sample accomplished all of the required activities in terms of observing, conferring, completing necessary forms, and so on. Substantively there was great variance in terms of how the program was carried out.... In cases where no strong team leadership appeared, the induction program seldom rose above the procedural compliance level. (p. 19)

These same researchers also noted an interesting point related to the gate-keeping function of teacher induction programs. From data secured from interviews with state officials in the two states it was indicated that nearly all of the teachers statewide enrolled in both programs were recommended for certification. They comment, "Such patterns would seem to call into question either the 'gate-keeping' capacity of such programs or the real need for such programs in the first place on the grounds of controlling for the quality of entering teachers" (Hoffman, Edwards, O'Neal, Barnes, and Paulissen 1986, p. 18).

Goal 5: To Transmit the Culture of the System to Beginning Teachers

As mentioned earlier, it appears that this goal is less prevalent in many programs than the other four. It appears that while many programs recognize that one program function is to "socialize" beginning teachers and to familiarize them with the workplace norms, the program stops far short of defining and transmitting the culture of the system. It can be speculated that locally developed programs more often tend to emphasize this "culture" goal than state-mandated programs in that local agencies are more likely to "own" a common culture which they want to transmit to the beginning teacher. In any case, the two studies which address this goal most directly are both locally developed programs.

The Ohio County School Teacher Induction Program in Wheeling, West Virginia, has as one of its objectives that teachers would develop a sense of ownership and bonding to an excellent system (Marockie and Looney 1988). In the evaluation report on the program, it states:

Results of evaluation of the Teacher Induction Program indicated that the program was extremely successful in guiding inductees in becoming bonded to the system and adopting the goals of the system. Through a positive interaction between central office personnel and

24

new teacher as well as principal and new teacher, ownership began to develop. Results seem to suggest that each teacher became more and more a part of the system and the sense of belonging to an excellent system became greater and greater. Out of the developing ownership emerged a real commitment to the system and the teacher's role in it. (pp. 2–3)

A similar phenomenon was described by Brooks (1986) in his work with the Richardson ISD (Texas) induction program. He wrote, "Beginning teacher reports of increased feelings of competence, motivation, belonging, support, and attention combine to produce an overwhelming perception of district competence and motivation to assist and develop entry year professionals" (p. 7). From this observation it can be inferred that the Richardson program has attempted to address the goal of transmitting the culture of the district to beginning teachers and has indeed accomplished this goal to a reasonably high degree.

It is possible that many developers and implementers of induction programs have not yet given much thought to the goal of transmitting the culture of the system to the beginning teacher. As more programs begin to incorporate this goal and report their results, it may be that greater numbers of those working in the field will begin to recognize the benefits of such a goal and to address it more directly in the future.

OTHER NOTEWORTHY FINDINGS

While the 17 studies included in this synthesis collectively include many more findings than have been discussed here, it is the author's hope that most of the major findings have been captured in the preceding sections of this [chapter]. However, the author believes there are four additional points that are clearly present in these studies that have not yet been discussed and are worth examining here. These four points include: the need for flexibility in induction programs, the important role of the support teacher, the importance of placement in beginning teacher success, and the need to educate both the profession and the public about teacher induction.

The Need for Flexibility in Induction Programs

Because beginning teachers are individuals, they will experience their first year of teaching and the induction process in individual, personal ways. In a study of the Virginia Beginning Teacher Assistance Program (Wildman, Niles, Magliaro, McLaughlin, and Drill 1987), a great deal of attention was given to this point. These researchers argue that is important to consider beginning teachers individually because their sources of problems, their ways of reacting and their aspirations for teaching can vary dramatically from person to person (p. 9).

Grant and Zeichner (1981) acknowledge the personal nature of teaching by noting that the problems and concerns experienced by the beginning teachers in their study were extremely diverse. They write:

> As Lewis (1980) argues, blanket statements about what to provide for first-year teachers are not very helpful. While general conclusions can be drawn about the necessity of more in-school support and better orientations, our data seem to indicate that the most useful thing that can be done with regard to induction is to personalize and individualize this support and gear it to the needs of the specific beginning teachers. (p. 110)

Huling-Austin, Putman, and Galvez-Hjornevik (1985) recommend that induction programs should be structured flexibly enough to accommodate the emerging needs of participants. They write:

> A prepackaged, "canned" program determined in advance will not be flexible enough to meet the variety of needs that are likely to emerge.... It is important to closely monitor the specific emerging needs and concerns of participants and to select appropriate interventions accordingly. By anticipating this need in advance it is possible to build in periodic assessments of the program and to plan at various points in the year to make adjustments in the types and amounts of assistance provided. (pp. 52–53)

The Important Role of the Support Teacher

Probably the most consistent finding across studies is the importance of the support teacher (sometimes called the mentor teacher, helping teacher, peer teacher, buddy teacher, etc.). Huling-Austin, Putnam, and Galvez-Hjornevik (1985) contend that, "The assignment of an appropriate support teacher is likely to be the most powerful and cost-effective intervention in an induction program" (p. 50). Most of the beginning teachers in their study reported that having a support teacher was the single most helpful aspect of the program because it gave them someone to turn to on a daily basis as problems arose.

The role of the support teacher or mentor teacher has probably been most carefully studied by the staff of the Center of Excellence in Teacher Education at Memphis State University. Butler (1987) outlined a number of personal factors which appeared to support the development of positive mentor-protege relationship. Some of these factors include: (1) prior experiences in assisting student teachers and novice teachers in understanding and mastering the responsibilities of teaching, (2) years of experience as a classroom teacher, (3) willingness to commit time to the protege early in the relationship so that both had opportunities to come to know and respect each other, (4) ability to conceive the relationship in developmental terms with sensitivity to the need to modify the mentor role as the protege progressed, and (5) possessing high status within the school and within the profession, such as attainment of higher rank on the state's career ladder program (pp. 3–4).

From their study of mentors, Huffman and Leak (1986) made the following two observations:

1. Having a mentor who teaches the same grade level or subject matter as the new teacher was highly desirable. In order to provide a full range of assistance, addressing issues including classroom management and instructional methodology as well as content, knowledge and experience in a similar discipline or grade level is important.

2. Providing adequate time for informal and formal conferencing, planning, and conversation between the mentor and the new teacher is a primary factor in addressing the needs of the beginners. Informal conferencing with the mentor was particularly valuable to these new teachers. (p. 24)

As to what exactly mentors do, the list of responsibilities, and activities is considerable. Huling-Austin and Murphy (1987) found that first-year teachers in their study reported receiving help from their support teachers in 14 different areas. Areas most frequently mentioned included "someone to talk to/listen to," followed by "locating materials" and "help with clerical work related to district policies and procedures." Other areas most frequently mentioned were "lesson planning," "classroom organization," and "discipline" (p. 33). Because the role of the support teacher is so extensive, Huling-Austin and Murphy recommend that support teachers should receive training in how to provide assistance in a variety of areas and in how to work with another adult in a supportive manner and should be compensated for their participation in induction programs (pp. 34–35).

Kilgore and Kozisek (1988) came to a similar conclusion from their study in which mentors were provided with neither training nor compensation. They concluded from their study that the role of the mentor teacher as envisioned was not fulfilled primarily because mentors were not provided with support for assuming the duties of a mentor (e.g., extra pay, recognition, training) by their principals. They concluded that, "The school as an organization has to come to grips with how they see mentors or career teachers helping those working their way into the system" (p. 12).

The Importance of Placement in Beginning Teacher Success

Beginning teachers are often placed in teaching assignments that would challenge even the most skillful veteran teachers. These difficult assignments can take several forms including teaching in a subject area for which the teacher is not certified, having numerous class preparations, "floating" from classroom to classroom, working with low-ability or unmotivated/disruptive students, or being responsible for demanding or time-consuming extracurricular activities.

Hidalgo (1987) recently completed a study of first-year teachers in difficult settings. His case studies give vivid accounts of novice emergency-credentialed teachers assigned to teach high-demand subjects in low-income, overcrowded junior high schools while they were still enrolled in teacher preparation classes. While certainly Hidalgo's subjects were in extremely challenging assignments, even less extreme circumstances can have major effects on the induction process, according to a number of different teacher induction researchers who have noted the importance of teaching assignment as it relates to beginning teacher success.

For example, in their study of two state-mandated programs, Hoffman and his colleagues (1986) noted:

> The programs appeared to work best when the teaching context was appropriate to the talents and interests of the first-year teacher. The programs did not provide sufficient support to overcome inappropriate placements or stressful work conditions., And, in fact, in such situations the programs only serve to further antagonize and exacerbate negative feelings. (p. 20)

In another study, Huling-Austin, Putman, and Galvez-Hjornevik (1985) came to a similar conclusion. They wrote:

> Placement of first-year teachers may well be the most influential variable in first-year teaching success. Which classes a first-year teacher is assigned to teach will be extremely influential in how successful a year that teacher is likely to have. The first-year teacher in our program who had the most difficulty was the one who had the most difficult teaching assignment both because not only were the students low achievers, but also her academic background had not prepared her to teach the

specific subject to which she was assigned. In comparison to other first-year teachers in the project, the teacher in the difficult assignment appeared weak. Our staff speculate that had this teacher been placed in a "less difficult" assignment or that the other first-year teachers had been placed in a similarly difficult assignment, that the resulting experiences may well have appeared quite different. The interventions supplied in the project were not sufficiently powerful enough to resolve the types of problems beginning teachers will experience in a difficult teaching assignment. (p. 48)

The Need to Educate the Profession (as well as the Public) about Teacher Induction

This final point, while it may appear to be obvious, is one that the author fears is being overlooked in our rush to implement induction programs across the nation. Many of us assume that because more legislatures are mandating induction programs and programs are rapidly increasing in number across the nation, that there must be general consensus in the profession at-large about the need and potential benefits of teacher induction programs. It is this author's experience that this is simply not the case. For example, in a recent presentation to teachers from more than 75 schools in Central Texas, not a single school had any type of induction program in operation (not even the assignment of a "buddy" teacher for new teachers). This evidence indicates that beginning teacher induction is not viewed as a pressing need in the field.

Kilgore and Kozisek (1988) comment on the same issue, "For the most part, school personnel are not aware of the literature or effects they have on first-year teachers. Simply stated, principals and teachers treat novice teachers like they were treated, and have had no reason to think that things should be any different" (p. 11).

If induction programs are to succeed, school practitioners need to be educated to the needs of beginning teachers and the role of experienced personnel in assisting with the induction process. In addition, those conducting induction programs need to be provided with the resources needed to fulfill these roles. If this information and support is not provided, induction programs have little chance of succeeding on a widespread basis. Friske and Combs (1986) perhaps summarized this point best:

Improving the quality of education can not merely be legislated. On paper, requirements can be met, yet still not effect true education reform. ... Without the commitment to the quality with which each (school practitioner) fulfills responsibilities to the beginning teacher and the teacher induction program, new teachers will merely be socialized into the existing system. (p. 72)

SUMMARY

The purpose of this [chapter] was to identify and synthesize findings from data-based research on teacher induction programs and practices. In order to be included in the synthesis studies must have been: (1) data based, (2) conducted on beginning teachers in an induction program, and (3) reported since 1977. A total of 17 studies were included in the synthesis.

Findings were organized around five common goals of teacher induction programs. An additional category was devoted to "Other Noteworthy Findings" for study that either did not clearly relate to one of the five goals or that cut across so many of the goals that it would be inappropriate to categorize them under a single goal. The organizing framework for the synthesis, therefore, include the following:

1. Goal 1: To improve teaching performance

2. Goal 2: To increase the retention of promising beginning teachers during the induction years

3. Goal 3: To promote the personal and professional well-being of beginning teachers

4. Goal 4: To satisfy mandated requirements related to induction and certification

5. Goal 5: To transmit the culture of the system to beginning teachers

6. Goal 6: Other Noteworthy Findings.

As this synthesis reflects, there is research data to support that induction programs can be successful in achieving each of the five goals stated above. In addition, the studies collectively include important findings about four other points: (1) the need for flexibility in induction programs, (2) the important role of the support teacher, (3) the importance of placement in beginning teacher success, and (4) the need to educate the profession (as well as the public) about teacher induction.

While there is evidence to suggest that induction programs can successfully achieve the goals outlined above, it is important for those who develop and implement programs to realize that for any of these goals to be achieved to any appreciable degree, program features and activities specifically targeted at addressing each goal must be planned and implemented. Program facilitators can make their own decisions about which goals to emphasize to what degree, but it is important to recognize that these goals will rarely be achieved "by accident" just because a program exists. In order for the goals to be achieved, program activities specifically targeted toward identified goals must be carefully designed and implemented appropriately.

REFERENCES

Arends, R. I. 1982. *Beginning teachers as learners: A descriptive report*. Paper presented at the annual meeting of the American Educational Research Association, New York.

Blackburn, J. 1977. *The first-year teacher: Perceived needs, intervention strategies and results*. Paper presented at the annual meeting of the American Educational Research Association, New York. ERIC No. ED 135 768.

Brooks, D. M. 1986. *Richardson new teacher induction program: Final data analysis and report*. Richardson, TX: Richardson ISD. ERIC No. ED 278 627.

_____. 1987. *Teacher induction: A new beginning*. Reston, VA: Association of Teacher Educators. ERIC No. 279 607.

Butler, E. D. 1987. *Lessons learned about mentoring in two fifth-year teacher preparation-induction programs*. Memphis: Memphis State University, Center of Excellence in Teacher Education. Paper presented at the annual meeting of the Association of Teacher Educators, Houston.

Elias, P.; McDonald, F. J.; Stevenson, C.; Simon, R.; and Fisher, M. L. 1980. *Study of induction programs for beginning teachers Vol. II: The problems of beginning teachers: A digest of helping programs*. Berkeley, CA: Educational Testing Service.

Elsner, K. 1984. *First year evaluation results from Oklahoma's entry-year assistance committees*. Paper presented at the annual meeting of the Association of Teacher Educators, New Orleans. ERIC No. 242 706.

Friske, J., and Combs, M. 1986. Teacher induction programs: An Oklahoma perspective. *Action in Teacher Education* 7 (2): 67–74.

Galvez-Hjornevik, C. 1985. *Teacher mentors: A review of the literature*. Austin: The University of Texas at Austin, The Research and Development Center for Teacher Education. ERIC No. ED 263 105.

Grant, C. A., and Zeichner, K. M. 1981. Inservice support for first year teachers: The state of the scene. *Journal of Research and Development in Education* 14 (2): 99-111.

Griffin, G. A. and Hukill, H. 1983. *First years of teaching: What are the pertinent issues?* Report No. 9051. Austin: The University of Texas at Austin, Research and Development Center for Teacher Education.

Hawk, P. P. 1984. *Making a difference: Reflections and thoughts of first year teachers*. Greenville, NC: East Carolina University.

Hegler, K., and Dudley, R. 1986. Beginning teacher induction: A progress report. *Journal of Teacher Education* 38 (1): 53–56.

Hidalgo, F. 1986–1987. The evolving concerns of first-year junior high school teachers in difficult settings: Three case studies. *Action in Teacher Education* 8 (4): 75–79.

Hoffman, J. V.; Edwards, S. A.; O'Neal, S.; Barnes, S.; and Paulissen, M. 1986. A study of state-mandated beginning teacher programs. *Journal of Teacher Education* 37 (1): 16–21.

Hord, S. M.; O'Neal, S. F.; and Smith, M. L., eds. 1985. *Beyond the looking glass: Papers from a national symposium on teacher education policies, practices and research*. Report No. 7203. Austin: The University of Texas at Austin, Research and Development Center for Teacher Education.

Huffman, G., and Leak, S. 1986. Beginning teachers' perceptions of mentors. *Journal of Teacher Education* 37 (1): 22–25.

Huling-Austin, L. 1988. *Teacher induction*. A speech presented to the South Texas Teacher Center, San Antonio, Texas, February 2, 1988.

_____. 1986. What can and cannot reasonably be expected from teacher induction programs. *Journal of Teacher Education* 37 (1): 2–5.

Huling-Austin, L., and Murphy, S. C. 1987. *Assessing the impact of teacher induction programs: Implications for program development*. Paper presented at the annual meeting of the American Educational Research Association, Washington, DC. ERIC No. 283 779.

Huling-Austin, L.; Putman, S.; Edwards, S.; and Galvez-Hjornevik, C. 1985. *MTIP satellite conference proceedings*. Report No. 7209. Austin: The University of Texas at Austin, Research and Development Center for Teacher Education.

Huling-Austin, L.; Putman, S.; and Galvez-Hjornevik, C. 1985. *Model teacher induction project study findings: Final report*. Austin: The University of Texas, Research and Development Center for Teacher Education. ERIC No. ED 270 442.

Johnston, J. M. 1988. *The knowledge base of teacher induction: A selected annotated bibliography*. Paper presented at the annual meeting of the Association of Teacher Educators, San Diego.

Kilgore, A. M., and Kozisek, J. A. 1988. *The effects of a planned induction program on first-year teachers: A research report*. Paper presented at the annual meeting of the Association of Teacher Educators, San Diego.

Lewis, C. 1980. Some essential characteristics of programs to support teachers in the beginning years. In *Toward meeting the needs of the beginning teacher*, ed. K. Howey and R. Bents. Minneapolis: USOE/Teacher Corps.

McCaleb, J. L. 1984. *An investigation of on-the-job performance of first-year teachers: Follow-up study.* College Park, MD: University of Maryland, Department of Curriculum and Instruction.

Marockie, M., and Looney, G. E. 1988. *Evaluating teacher induction in Ohio County Schools, Wheeling, West Virginia.* Paper presented at the annual meeting of the Association of Teacher Educators, San Diego.

Odell, S. J. 1986. Induction support of new teachers: A functional approach. *Journal of Teacher Education* 37 (1): 26–29.

Ryan, K.; Newman, K.; Mager, G.; Applegate, J.; Lasley, T.; Flora, R.; and Johnston, J. 1980. *Biting the apple: Accounts of first year teachers.* New York: Longman.

Schlechty, P., and Vance, V. 1983. Recruitment, selection and retention: The shape of the teaching force. *The Elementary School Journal* 83 (4): 468–87.

Summers, J. A. 1987. *Summative evaluation report: Project CREDIT.* Terre Haute, Indiana State University, School of Education.

Wildman, T. M.; Niles, J. A.; Magliaro, S. G.; McLaughlin, R. A.; and Drill, L. G. 1987. *Virginia's colleague teacher project: Focus on beginning teachers' adaptation to teaching.* Paper presented at the annual meeting of the American Educational Research Association, Washington, DC.

3. SCHOOL-BUILDING-LEVEL VARIABLES AND THE INDUCTION OF NEW TEACHERS

by James D. Greenberg and Maurice C. Erly

I have a first-year English teacher who has three different levels of seventh grade, two levels of eighth grade, and five different literature books; and I've seen her panic a lot.

—Sylvia, experienced teacher on beginning
teacher task force, 3/26/87

The perplexing condition observed by Sylvia, the experienced teacher quoted above, is all too common. Anyone who is now or has ever been a classroom teacher probably experienced a similar sense of being overloaded and overwhelmed—either directly or through the troubles of a colleague. Yet, while the recognition of this sort of new teacher problem is almost universal among school professionals, scholars, and researchers who have contributed to the literature on induction have given relatively little emphasis to these "facts of life." When they do, the stress often seems to be on the needs of the beginning teacher to learn to cope with her/his new reality, the support available from workshops on classroom management, effective instruction, or the advice of a mentor, or the deficiencies of preservice programs that were supposed to prepare them "more realistically" anyway. Accordingly, the remedies most often discussed appear to be programmatic in nature, i.e., training programs, mentor programs, staff development programs, induction programs—all in support of the new teacher.

However, the category of concerns illustrated in Sylvia's opening quote—referred to alternatively as "situational variables," "context variables," and the like—are often overlooked, taken for granted, or merely identified as problems requiring more attention. Nor have the logical solutions to some of these problems, namely, policy and administrative decisions of principals and central office supervisory personnel, been examined for their potential role in relation to better induction efforts. Indeed, as the present authors have stated previously, negative context variables—and the decisions that helped to create them—seriously affect the potential success chances for beginning teachers.

34

It is one of the most reprehensible yet persistent realities that decision makers in education give beginning teachers hard initial assignments. Such decisions are not made usually because the new teacher has requested such an assignment, or because an administrator is trying to apply some consciously conceived test of competence. Rather, it is more likely that such decisions are made out of convenience and/or on the basis of a priority system that places seniority and rank above competency match factors when designing individual job assignments. While this condition has been verbally assailed over the years, little has changed in practice. (Erly and Greenberg 1985)

PURPOSE AND METHODOLOGY

The purpose of the data collection and research effort reported here was to investigate the current status of school building level context variables in a large school system that has made concerted attempts to improve recruiting and retention procedures. Induction concerns have been addressed to a degree and continue to be addressed in this school system. Yet, no data existed regarding the perceptions of new teachers in terms of the school building environments in which they were placed, or about some of the administrative decisions and assignments that have been noted to affect the quality and potential success of the induction period. These areas are among the least studied in the literature, yet they represent the kinds of things that may be affected and improved simply by a change of will, attitude, or policy—often without any direct economic cost involved.

The method of data collection was a questionnaire, administered to 368 teachers hired into the school system at the beginning of (or during) the 1986–1987 academic year. The questionnaire method was chosen because it was the most efficient way to obtain a large amount of baseline data that could serve as a foundation for further in-depth study. Another reason was related to the opportunity to include questions relevant to the purpose of this study in a comprehensive instrument that could be directly administered to three large groups of new teachers who would come together for day-long staff development meetings during the second semester of the academic year. The potential for very high percentage returns, and the need to avoid overloading the subject population, reinforced the choice of methodology.

The sample surveyed included 368 teachers hired into the school system sometime during the current academic year. These new teachers represented all teaching fields and levels, and included those with prior experience in other geographic areas, prior experience in this school system

35

and now returning after a period of absence, and beginning teachers with no prior experience save their student teaching. Data were sought from this sample of new teachers in the following areas:

1. *Demographic variables.* Data were requested related to sex, age, date hired, class size, years taught, years since last taught (both in this system, or in another school or school system), grade level taught, secondary content area (if any). The purpose of obtaining the demographic data was to have the ability to analyze responses according to the variables noted, and to determine whether response differences related to those variables.

2. *Areas and levels of concern.* A list of areas of concern was drawn from the literature. The items on the list were those that were often reported as being concern areas for new teachers, and they were almost all items pertinent to school building level variables. The purpose was to see whether this large sample, in this particular school system, had these concerns as they reflected on their initial year and, if so, what degree of seriousness accompanied the concern.

3. *Committee assignments and extra duties.* Respondents were asked to list those committee assignments and extra duties they had been given in order to determine load and type of assignment in this category. As the literature suggests, this is an important area of "overload" for new teachers, and as these matters are almost certainly under the control of building level decisions, this information was requested as a separate item.

4. *Respondents were asked to write brief descriptions* of three things that helped them at the building level, three things that did not help, or hindered them, at the building level, and three things that they wished had been done at the building level to help, but weren't. Other comments were also requested.

RESULTS AND IMPLICATIONS

The results obtained from the questionnaires are reported here at a quite fundamental level of analysis. However, these first analyses and displays of data prove quite interesting as a start. In Table 1, the levels of concern data are presented for all items that respondents were given. No item was rated as a concern by less than 57 percent of the respondents; and no item was rated by more than 83 percent (NOTE: Some individual items were not marked by certain respondents, so total respon-

Table 1
Level of Concern Expressed for 14 School Building Variables

	Level of Concern:										
	1		2		3		4		5		
Item Number					Respondents Report:						Total[a]
and Category	No.	%	No.	%	No.	%	No.	%	No.	%	No.
38 Orientation	41	27.0	29	11.0	75	28.5	60	22.8	28	10.6	263
39 Space	43	15.2	31	11.0	80	28.4	58	20.6	70	24.8	282
40 Time	28	9.6	28	9.6	68	23.2	83	28.3	86	29.4	293
41 Assignment	56	23.3	31	12.9	53	22.1	53	22.1	47	19.6	240
42 Resources	30	9.8	35	11.4	80	26.1	71	23.2	90	29.4	306
43 Class size	38	13.3	22	7.7	71	24.9	60	21.1	94	33.0	285
44 Student performance	22	7.6	29	10.0	74	25.5	78	26.9	87	30.0	296
45 Assistance	38	13.8	34	12.4	70	25.5	73	26.5	60	21.8	275
46 Administrative duties	23	8.3	45	16.3	77	27.7	77	27.7	54	19.6	276
47 Lesson planning	35	13.7	29	11.3	65	25.4	64	25.0	63	24.6	251
48 Extra duties	39	15.7	36	14.5	76	30.5	43	17.3	55	22.1	249
49 Opportunity to observe	30	11.3	22	12.0	65	24.4	71	25.7	68	25.6	266
50 Teaming opportunity	39	15.5	28	11.1	59	23.4	58	23.0	68	27.0	252
51 Collegial relationships	40	19.2	27	13.0	58	27.9	37	17.8	46	22.1	208

[a] Total Number = 368. Those not reporting are assumed to have no concern for the item.

dents do not equal 100 percent for each item.) The top three areas of concern, in terms of frequency of citation, were related to resources, student performance, and time. However, when viewed according to level of seriousness expressed about the concern, the top three areas (rated according to combined responses of 3, 4, and 5 on the scale of seriousness of concern) were the same as those noted for frequency, but the order changed, with time and student performance tied for first place and resources third. The results further show that quite a few areas are scored as fairly serious concerns by the majority of respondents, and the data may help building administrators and staff attend to the particular concerns as they are manifested in various individual buildings.

Table 2 reports the results of extra duties and committee assignments listed by respondents. According to this self-report, the largest number of new teachers have been given no additional duties beyond their regular teaching (and teaching-related) loads. However, 127 new teachers report two or more such assignments or responsibilities. The contrast, and the range of assignments reported, suggest that more needs to be learned about who is being assigned these additional duties, and why. While credit should be given to building administrators who have protected the largest single group of new teachers from all additional duties, many others apparently did not. This is a "classic" area cited for destructive effects on the new teacher, and a number of new teachers reporting extra duties noted that this was a serious concern for them.

Tables 3, 4, and 5 report the specific areas cited by respondents as helps, hindrances, and desirable changes in relation to their own school building. The categories were derived from a rough content analysis of written comments under each question area in the survey. The categories conformed well to the kinds of variables reported in the literature as significant and relevant.

Of most dramatic interest, and perhaps of most importance, is the utterly clear priority given to "people" matters in the citations of examples of positive assistance. In the area of helps (Table 3), the mentions related to helpful and cooperative administrators and colleagues in the building so overshadowed the rest of the items that the closest "competitor," namely the area of resources, was hardly noticeable. Administration and staff help was mentioned eight times more than resources and over 13 times more frequently than logistical considerations, the third most frequent area cited.

However, the picture changes—and the spread is much greater—in the "hindrance" and "wishes" domains. Administrative logistics heads the list of negative citation categories (see Table 4), and that would include the matters of misassignment, multiple preparations, nonperma-

Table 2
Extra Duties and Committee Assignments Reported

Number of Committee and Extra Duties Reported	Number of Respondents Reporting
0	91
1	33
2	50
3	27
4	30
5	5
6 or more	15

Table 3
School Building Items Reported as Helpful (N=368)

Item Category and Descriptors	Number Reporting
Time (helpful meetings; released time)	0
Parents (supportive, etc.)	3
Students (positive; motivated; enjoyable)	1
Materials and supplies (resources)	50
Administration/Staff (helpful; cooperative)	403
Program (workshops; orientation)	20
Communication	2
Administrative logistics (space; schedule)	30
Miscellaneous	2
Systemwide helps[a]	4

[a] This was not requested reference level for response, but a few reported items at this level.

Table 4
School Building Items Reported as Hindrances (N=368)

Item Category and Descriptors	Number Reporting
Time demands (interruptions; too many meetings, etc.)	38
Parents (overly demanding, etc.)	5
Students (difficult; unmotivated)	26
Materials and supplies (inadequate; poor quality)	85
Administration/Staff (negative; nonsupportive; uncooperative; threatening)	97
Program (lack of orientation; instruction on testing, etc)	23
Extra duties and assignments	18
Communication (poor)	16
Administrative logistics (space; schedule, etc.)	145
Miscellaneous	5
Systemwide matters	4

nent or inadequate classroom and other space, and difficult schedules, interruptions, administrative demands, and so on. It is this very category that many observers are coming to realize has the most potential for amelioration within the induction arena; yet, probably because it is not considered staff development or training, or because it doesn't fit in the target most induction efforts have assumed they must aim at—namely, the needs/deficiencies of the novice—there has been little attention given to the integral nature of administrative decisions in relation to potential success of induction programs. While much more specificity is needed regarding the data on this item, preliminary indications are that the most serious hindrance to new teacher success could be substantially alleviated by administrative process and choices at the school building level. Such an interpretation may be reinforced by the recognition that the second most cited hindrance category is the one reflecting administration and staff nonsupport and the negative climate and morale decline that accompanies such a perspective.

The data on wishes (Table 5) also reflect a range of concerns, and implied suggestions, and no single category dramatically outdistances the rest. As expected from the citation of administrative logistics as the category perceived to be the greatest hindrance, respondents noted that area as the one they most wished would be improved in the future. Close behind, however, was the notation by 55 respondents that more program provision would have been desirable. Orientation, information and skill development in testing procedures and preparation, and instructional improvement assistance were items included by respondents who wrote on this category. It is assumed that requests related to building level program help, both for the sake of relevance and accessibility. Coupled with the overwhelming frequency of citations regarding administrator and colleague support as significant help received, it seems clear that mentor

---

Table 5
School Building Areas Wished for Improvement

Item Category and Descriptors	Number Reporting
Time (more; better allocated)	15
Parents (more helpful)	2
Students (better; more positive)	5
Materials and supplies (better and more)	32
Administration/staff (more positive; help more)	37
Program (more and better)	55
Communication (better)	12
Administrative logistics (better schedule/assignment; better space, etc.)	67
Miscellaneous	8
Systemwide matters	2

arrangements, and/or school-based team support arrangements, could provide both the personal and program support structure needed and valued by new teachers.

SUMMARY, CONCLUSIONS, AND RECOMMENDATIONS

There is still much that needs to be done with the data collected in this study. Demographic variables need to be analyzed in relation to the results reported in order to determine whether any (e.g., date of employment, years of prior experience, teaching level) appear to differentiate on some of the variables studied. It would make a great difference, for example, that the new teachers who reported lots of extra duty assignments were experienced in another system as opposed to being brand new teachers right out of undergraduate teacher education programs. Similarly, it would be instructive if most of the concerns about resources, or about misassignment, came from secondary as opposed to elementary teachers. Given such finer "cuts" on the data, the value and utility of the information for decision makers and staff developers could increase substantially.

Another step for future study would be to interview a sample of respondents in order to gain enriched perspective on the meaning and the implications of the data collected in this study. Much of the analysis and interpretation would be greatly enhanced by checking perceptions and reasoning behind some of the choices made on the levels of concern component, and by learning more detail about the kinds of administrative decisions and behaviors perceived to be particularly supportive and helpful as well as those perceived to be detrimental and destructive in the induction period.

Finally, it appears that there is reason to believe that much hope can be Placed in the potential for improving the "induction system" by paying attention to school level context variables, and the decisions and choices that can cause such variables to be seen as supportive of successful induction or, conversely, as detrimental to it. While traditional forms of assistance will always be important parts of a comprehensive induction program, insights into what makes school buildings supportive of new teachers can be an enormous contribution to establishing contexts that can make induction into the profession a positive process.

REFERENCE

Erly, M., and Greenberg, J. 1985. A collaborative proposal for a multi-level induction process. International Seminar in Teacher Education for the 80s and 90s, Leira, Portugal.

41

4. CHARACTERISTICS OF BEGINNING TEACHERS IN AN INDUCTION CONTEXT*

by Sandra J. Odell

Structured teacher induction programs have emerged across the country. Eleven states have mandated induction programs for all school districts, and 21 other states are either piloting or planning statewide induction efforts (Hawk and Robards 1987). As induction programs continue to emerge, it becomes increasingly important to characterize fully the beginning teacher within an induction context.

Our previous research has been directed toward identifying those needs that are unique to beginning teachers undergoing induction to the teaching profession. This has been accomplished by observing the actual functioning of an elementary induction support program (Odell 1986b), by recording the questions new elementary teachers ask of induction support personnel across their first year of teaching (Odell, Loughlin, and Ferraro 1987), and by identifying the developmental level of teaching for new teachers using a Stages of Concerns questionnaire (Odell 1987). In general, this research has served to characterize the evolution of the new teacher and tentatively to define the types of support needed in the induction of developing teachers.

The present research used the interview method to describe further the characteristics of new elementary teachers in an induction context. In particular, the research was designed (1) to reveal new teacher motivations, attitudes, and expectations; (2) to identify the concerns of beginning teachers and the support personnel most helpful to beginning teachers; (3) to assess the impact of the teaching context on the first year of teaching; and (4) to reveal what changes in teacher practice new teachers would make in a new year.

---

*The author expresses her appreciation to the clinical support teachers, especially Nancy Cole and Shirley McGuire, who collected and helped analyze data for this study and, importantly, who helped the first-year teachers to become better instructional leaders.

PROCEDURE

The data were obtained within the context of a large-scale elementary school teacher induction program that is a collaborative effort between a college of education and a major school district (Odell 1986a). The subjects were 18 teachers, 16 females, and 2 males, who were drawn randomly from 180 first-year elementary teachers receiving weekly induction support from 9 clinical support teachers. The clinical support teachers were veteran classroom teachers who were released from classroom duties in order to work full time assisting the 180 beginning teachers. The 18 beginning teachers chosen for this study were all recent graduates holding baccalaureate degrees in elementary education.

During the course of the school year, the clinical support teachers administered an interview three times to the 18 beginning teachers: during the first two weeks of school, after the midyear holiday break, and in the last month of school. On the average, an interview took approximately 30 minutes to complete.

The interview consisted of seven open-ended questions that were read to the beginning teachers by a clinical support teacher. Four of the seven questions were asked in each of the three interviews, while the remaining three questions varied across the interviews. Each of the resultant interview questions was assumed to access one of the following seven characteristics: teacher motivation, teacher attitude, new teacher expectations, new teacher needs, sources of new teacher support, the impact of the teaching context, or teaching practice. The verbatim interview questions and teaching characteristics are listed in Table 1. Teacher responses to questions related to new teacher challenges/concerns were further subdivided into seven categories of needed support based on those used in a previous study, as shown in Table 2 (Odell, Loughlin, and Ferraro 1987).

The interviews were tape-recorded for later transcription and analysis. Teacher responses to the questions as recorded and transcribed were then tallied using verbatim phrases so as to create a description of new teachers in an induction context.

RESULTS

In order to summarize the responses to the teacher motivation, teacher attitude, teacher expectation, sources of new teacher support, teaching context, and teaching practice questions, the percentage of subjects giving a particular response was determined.

With respect to teacher motivation, during Interview I, nine different reasons were given by the 18 subjects for becoming a teacher. Enjoyment of children or school was cited by 66.7 percent of the new teachers, and

Table 1
Teaching Characteristics Accessed by Individual Interview Questions
During Interviews, I, II, or III

Teaching Characteristics	Interview Questions
Motivation	
Interview I	Why did you decide to become a teacher?
Attitude	
Interview II	How do you feel about your decision to become a teacher?
Interview III	If you had it to do over again, would you decide to become a teacher?
Teacher practice	
Interview III	What would you do differently in a new year?
Challenges	
Interviews I, II	Currently, what are your biggest challenges?
Support personnel	
Interviews, I, II	Who has been helpful in dealing with the challenges?
Interviews I, II, III	Who has been the most helpful so far?
Concerns	
Interviews I, II, III	What concerns you the most right now?
Expectations	
Interviews I, II, III	In what ways has teaching been similar to or different from what you expected?
Context	
Interviews I, II, III	What about this school or community makes teaching particularly easy or difficult?

was the most frequently cited motivation. Wanting to be a teacher since childhood was mentioned by 22.2 percent and 16.7 percent mentioned being motivated by previous teachers of their own. The remaining responses were more individualistic and followed no discernible trend.

In general, the new teacher attitude questions revealed that the new teachers had very positive feelings about teaching. In Interview II, teachers were asked how they felt about their decision to be a teacher. All teachers but one responded positively with comments such as: "feels good," "right choice," "enjoy the profession," and "satisfied." The one other teacher said that she felt "good and bad depending on the day." Interview III revealed a similarly positive attitude about teaching, with 100 percent of the new teachers saying that they would decide to be

Table 2
Categories of Needed Support Used to Characterize
Challenges and Concerns of New Teachers

Example Challenge/ Concern	Needed Support Category	Description of Support Category
Individualizing math activities	Instruction	Giving information to new teachers about teaching strategies
Meeting administrative expectations	System	Giving information to new teachers related to procedures and guidelines of the school district
Accumulating teaching materials	Resource	Collecting, disseminating, or locating resources for use by new teachers
Surviving the first year	Emotional	Offering new teachers personal support through empathic listening and by sharing experiences
Time allocation for instruction	Managerial	Helping new teachers manage and organize the school day
Dealing with parental expectations	Parental	Giving new teachers help with ideas related to conferencing with parents
Maintaining control	Discipline	Giving new teachers ideas related to managing children

a teacher if they had it to do over again. The expanded answers to this question, such as "Teaching is challenging," "I love working with the kids," and "I find teaching rewarding," also suggested uniformly positive attitudes about teaching.

The teacher expectation question revealed that subjects more often say that teaching is different than they expected than they say that it is the same as expected. Specifically, responses that teaching is different than expected encompassed 88.5 percent, 94.4 percent, and 76.2 percent of all the expectation responses in Interviews I, II, and III, respectively. Subjects were less consistent regarding the particular ways that teaching is different than they expected. In Interview I, 33 percent of the subjects said that teaching is more difficult than they expected, and 16.7 percent listed classroom management as different than expected. The remaining responses specifically identifying the ways that teaching is different were quite variable and mentioned by only one new teacher. In Interview II, 16.7 percent of the subjects listed time management as more difficult than expected. In Interview III, 16.7 percent of the subjects responded that the work was harder than expected. All other responses to the expectation question in Interviews II and III were completely individual and demonstrated no particular pattern of response.

Sources of support for new teachers were determined through two questions in Interviews I and II and through one question in Interview III. In response to the question of who has been helpful in dealing with challenges and concerns faced by the new teachers, colleague teachers were identified by 58.4 percent, 55.6 percent, and 50 percent of the subjects, clinical support teachers were identified by 44.7 percent, 58.3 percent, and 83.3 percent of the subjects, and principals were listed by 13.9 percent, 13.9 percent, and 33.3 percent of the subjects in Interviews I, II, and III, respectively. Several other sources of support in dealing with concerns and facing challenges were identified but were listed by no more than one subject. There was a tendency, however, to list family members such as mother, spouse, and brother.

The impact of the teaching context on teaching was explored in all three interviews by asking teachers whether there was anything about their school or community that makes teaching particularly easy or difficult. In all three interviews, responses included factors that make teaching difficult. Parent or family difficulties comprised 36 percent of the 14 factors listed in Interview I, 46 percent of the 13 factors listed in Interview II, and 100 percent of the seven factors listed in Interview III. No other factors related to difficulty were listed more than once. In terms of the factors that make teaching particularly easy, the modal factor in Interviews I, II, and III, respectively, was staff support (33.3%), parental support (45.4%), and principal support (41.2%).

One teacher-practice question, "What will you do differently next year?" was asked in Interview III. There were a total of 26 responses from the 18 new teachers, 50 percent of which were related directly to instruction (e.g., "restructure the reading program," "plan more small-group instruction," "individualize instruction more"). The other 50 percent of the responses were related to changes the new teachers would make in their own behaviors (e.g., "relax more," "be more flexible," "set higher expectations for children").

New-teacher needs were determined through two questions in each of the three interviews. The responses to the questions of what are your biggest challenges and concerns were subdivided into seven categories of needed support, as shown previously in Table 2. Table 3 lists the percentage of responses in each of the seven need categories for all three interviews, as well as the mean percent responses for the three interviews combined.

Table 3
Percentage of Challenge and Concern Responses Made by
New Teachers in Each Category of Needed Support for Each Interview
and for the Mean of the Three Interviews Combined

Needed Support Category	Interview I	Interview II	Interview III	Mean Percent
Instruction	36.4	56.8	45.8	46.3
System	9.9	2.8	20.8	11.2
Resource	3.7	0.0	0.0	1.2
Emotional	3.9	2.8	6.2	4.3
Managerial	23.3	13.4	8.3	15.0
Parental	5.9	5.5	6.3	5.9
Discipline	17.1	18.7	12.5	16.1

By way of overview, instructional needs were identified most frequently in each interview, occurring 36.4 percent, 56.8 percent, and 45.8 percent of the time in Interviews I, II, and III, respectively. System needs fell from 9.9 percent in Interview I to only 2.8 percent in Interview II, but increased to 20.8 percent in Interview III as the new teachers evinced concern over their job status for the ensuing school year. The resource, emotional, and parental categories received less focus with all percentages falling below 7 percent. Management needs were identified frequently during Interview I (23.3%) and declined over time in Interviews II (13.4%) and III (8.3%) as teachers presumably became more effective in organizing the school day. Needs related to discipline remained fairly stable from Interview I (17.1%) to Interview II (18.7%), but fell somewhat at Interview III (12.5%).

DISCUSSION

The data presented above, obtained in a teacher induction context, indicate that the majority of teachers are motivated to begin teaching by their enjoyment of children and school and that they maintain a very positive attitude about teaching across the induction year. Indeed, all of the new teachers at the end of their first year said that they would decide to begin teaching if they had that decision to make over again. This is encouraging, given the disturbing statistic that 15 percent of new teachers not in structured induction programs leave the profession after the first year (Schlechty and Vance 1983).

Over the past several years, there has been considerable attention given to the perils of beginning teaching (Glassberg 1979; Sprinthall and Thies-Sprinthall 1983; Veenman 1984). More specifically, teachers entering the profession without induction support suffer "reality shock," in which there is a collapse of ideals formed in the process of teacher training, under the tremendous pressures of classroom teaching. It is a tribute to the concept of teacher induction that the new teachers in this program maintained a very positive attitude about teaching. This may be because the induction support offered to the new teachers served to lessen the teaching pressures they experienced. Almost all of the new teachers did say, however, that teaching is different from what they had expected in that teaching and aspects of time management were considerably more difficult than they had anticipated.

All of the new teachers found a variety of sources of support in dealing with the concerns and challenges they face. Somewhat more than half of the teachers found support in their teaching colleagues throughout the school year, although the influence of these colleagues declined some across time. Interestingly, the clinical support teachers became increasingly relied upon for support as the school year progressed, with more than 80 percent of the teachers using them as a source of support at the end of the school year. School principals were also seen as supportive by some of the teachers, but overall, school principals were not viewed as a particularly strong source of support by the new teachers.

First-year teachers are often uncomfortable with those in evaluative positions (Fox and Singletary 1986). In a study by Huffman and Leak (1986), new teachers viewed support personnel as "friendly critics" offering beneficial feedback and constructive criticism only if the support personnel were not in a formal evaluative role. In the present induction context, clinical support teachers were not involved in the evaluative process. Accordingly, it is not surprising that the clinical support teachers, who were offering assistance without assessment were identified by the new teachers as ultimately the most supportive in helping to meet the challenges and concerns of beginning teaching.

With respect to the teaching context, parental and family difficulties clearly represent a negative contextual factor for the major number of new teachers. This widely recognized contextual adversity is not completely ameliorated by a teacher induction context, and most likely will not be eliminated altogether in the absence of broader social change.

Of the significant categories of support needed by the new teachers that were revealed in the present interviews, two changed across time in predictable fashions. Support relating to administrative procedures of the school district was more needed at the end of the school year as teachers became concerned about their future employment. Support in managing and organizing the school day was most needed at the beginning of the school year and became less important at the end of the year when the new teachers had gained experience as a classroom instructional leader.

The two most frequently identified needs of the new teachers, those of support in the instructional process and in managing children, remained evident across the school year. In our previous research, the needs of new teachers in an induction context were assessed by observing the nature of support offered to new teachers by clinical support teachers (Odell 1986b), and by recording the questions that new teachers asked of clinical support teachers across their first year of teaching (Odell, Loughlin, and Ferraro 1987). Both of these approaches yielded data consistent with the present interview data in finding that supporting new teachers in the instructional process is far and away the most critical aspect of a teacher induction program.

On the other hand, the prior research found that new teachers only infrequently asked clinical support teachers for guidance and ideas related to managing children and that clinical support teachers rarely offered new teachers spontaneous discipline support as compared to other categories of support. These data clearly indicated that discipline does not represent a major concern of new teachers. This conclusion is at odds with other data obtained using an interview procedure (Veenman 1984), including the present interview data, which show that discipline is a concern of major proportions to the new teacher. It may well be that the various methods of assessing the needs of beginning teachers in an induction context tap different dimensions of teacher needs. For example, the previously used direct observational approaches may be primarily recording the frequency of needed teacher support, while the present post hoc interview procedure may be primarily assessing the intensity of teacher concerns. In other words, discipline problems may not occur with a very high frequency for the new teacher, but when they do, they may be perceived by the new teacher to be of considerable intensity.

The present data do not directly reveal whether the characteristics of new teachers in an induction context differ substantially from those of new teachers not receiving structured induction support. However, in contrasting the present induction context data with the general literature pertaining to the characteristics of new teachers (e.g., Hawk 1984; Lortie 1975; Ryan et al. 1980), it would appear that the teacher induction context may produce new teachers who are characterized as being more motivated to continue teaching, more open to the receipt of support, and more focused on the instructional process during their initial teaching year.

REFERENCES

Feiman-Nemser, S.; Odell, S. J.; and Lawrence, D. 1988. Induction programs and the professionalization of teachers: Two views. *Colloquy* 1 (2): 11–19.

Fox S. M., and Singletary, T. J. 1986. Deductions about supportive induction. *Journal of Teacher Education* 37 (1): 12–15.

Glassberg, S. 1979. A developmental model for the beginning teacher. In *Toward meeting the needs of the beginning teacher*, ed. K. R. Howey and R. H. Bents. Lansing, MI: Midwest Teacher Corps. Network. ERIC No. ED 206 581.

Hawk, P. 1984. *Making a difference: Reflections and thoughts of first-year teachers*. Greenville, NC: P. P. Hawk.

Hawk, P., and Robards, S. 1987. Statewide teacher induction programs. In *Teacher induction: A new beginning*, ed. D. M. Brooks. Reston, VA: Association of Teacher Educators.

Huffman, G., and Leak, S. 1986. Beginning teachers' perceptions of mentors. *Journal of Teacher Education* 37 (1): 16–21.

Lortie, D. D. 1975. *Schoolteacher: A sociological study*. Chicago: University of Chicago Press.

Odell, S. J. 1986a. A model university-school system collaboration in teacher induction. *Kappa Delta Pi Record* 22 (54): 120–21.

————. 1986b. Induction support of new teachers: A functional approach. *Journal of Teacher Education* 37 (1): 26–29.

————. 1987. *Stages of concern of beginning teachers in a collaborative internship/induction program*. Paper presented at the annual meeting of the Association of Teacher Educators, Houston, TX.

Odell, S. J.; Loughlin, C. E.; and Ferraro, D. P. 1987. Functional approach to identification of new teacher needs in an induction context. *Action in Teacher Education* 8 (4): 51–57.

Ryan, D.; Newman, K.; Mager, G.; Applegate, J.; Lasley, T.; Flora, R.; and Johnston, J. 1980. *Biting the apple: Accounts of first year teachers*. New York: Longman.

Schlechty, P., and Vance, V. 1983. Recruitment, selection and retention: The shape of the teaching force. *The Elementary School Journal* 83 (4): 469–87.

Sprinthall, N. A., and Thies-Sprinthall, L. 1983. The teacher as an adult learner: A cognitive-developmental view. In *Staff development*, ed. G. A. Griffin, Eighty-second Yearbook of the National Society for the Study of Education. Chicago: University of Chicago Press, 13–35.

Veenman, S. 1984. Perceived problems of beginning teachers. *Review of Educational Research* 54 (2): 143–78.

5. PROVIDING EFFECTIVE INDUCTION PROGRAM SUPPORT TEACHERS: IT'S NOT AS EASY AS IT LOOKS

by Louise Bay Waters and Victoria L. Bernhardt

Variously called "consulting teachers," "teacher consultants," or "support teachers," experienced teachers paired with novices is one of the most common elements of induction programs (Hoffman et al. 1986). According to Huling-Austin, Putman, and Galvez-Hjornevik (1985, p. 50), "The assignment of an appropriate support teacher is likely to be the most powerful and cost-effective intervention in an induction program." However, the potential effectiveness and apparent ready availability and low cost of support teachers masks the complexity of designing this important induction program feature. Without care in the initial program design, support teacher effectiveness is likely to be variable (Ward and Tikunoff 1987) and difficult to sustain over time. In this chapter, we present the optimal induction support by experienced teachers as taking place when there is a convergence of appropriate and reinforcing role expectations, training (in-service) programs, incentive plans, and selection procedure. Unfortunately, there are dilemmas in each of these areas that constrain the ability of a given program to implement what might potentially be the most effective type of consulting teacher support. In general, these dilemmas involve tensions between certain types of effectiveness and ease of implementation.

The problems inherent in the design of training programs, incentive plans, and selection procedures for support teachers will be detailed in the sections that follow. First, though, we will delineate a variety of potential roles for these teachers. It is the definition of these roles that provides the parameters for the design of the training component. In turn, the role definition and training expectations have significant implications for incentives and selection.

DEFINING THE ROLE OF THE SUPPORT TEACHER

As detailed in Table 1, the support teacher role can encompass a wide range of features. In general, these can be categorized as providing orientation and resources; psychological support; curriculum and instructional

Role Expectations	Focus of Training	Implications for Incentive Plan	Criteria for Selection
Table 1
The Interrelation of Support Teacher Role Expectations,
Training, Incentives, and Selections

Role Expectations	Focus of Training	Implications for Incentive Plan	Criteria for Selection
Orientation	Handbook/reference material		Experience in district and site
Psychological support	Coaching		Appropriate personality, proximity, confidentiality
Instructional advice		If support is informal and limited to these areas, fewer incentives needed	
Curricular advice			Match in subject, grade, proximity, excellent teaching skills
Modeling		Need released time	Willingness to be observed
Observation and feedback	Supervision (clinical)	Need released time	Ability to be facilitative, confidentiality
Implementation of a specific instructional program (i.e., M. Hunter, C. M. Charles, cooperative learning)	Specific methods of program	Time consuming, will probably require greater incentives	Interest and ability in program focus
Assessment	Assessment implementation	Can conflict with teacher contract	Willingness to assess, fairness, reliability

advice; classroom modeling; observation and feedback; assistance in implementing a specific instructional program; and assessment. Within each of these broad categories are a variety of options more specifically defining the type of service consultants provide.

Historically, schools have recognized the need to provide some type of new teacher orientation. *Orientation* to the school and district is still needed and, when support teachers can be chosen prior to the beginning of the school year, this person is the logical one to provide it. However, even when teacher consultants are not involved in initial orientation, orientation-like support is an important aspect of their role throughout the year. In this role they may direct new teachers to district resources, clarifying who to see about what and how to seek information in a way that is likely to get results.

The second type of assistance provided by experienced teachers is *psychological support*. Induction programs frequently see the consulting teacher as the one person most involved with helping the new teacher handle the reality shock of being totally responsible for teaching a group(s) of children for the first time. Many beginning teachers are not prepared for the stress, time demands, and isolation of their first job (Marso and Pigge 1986). Almost universally, they have difficulties with some aspect of classroom management and question their suitability for the profession (Gray and Gray 1985). The psychological support provided by the consulting teacher is, at the very least, a shoulder to cry on and a well-timed pep talk ("You're better than I was when I first started."). It can also involve helping the new teacher learn to balance personal life and work demands to keep from burning out (Wildman et al. 1987). Critical to psychological support is trust and confidentiality.

Consulting teachers are also a *source of advice on curriculum and instruction*. Most commonly this involves pragmatic, how-to advice (i.e., classroom management tips, how to set up grade books, ideas for teaching fractions). Relatedly, it can also include the sharing of resources such as lab equipment, math games, or read-aloud stories (Huling-Austin and Murphy 1987). In some induction programs, the involvement of teacher consultants in curriculum and instruction is much more formalized and entails *classroom observations and feedback* using coaching and/or clinical supervision techniques. Such programs often provide opportunities for consultants to *model* instructional techniques in their own or the new teacher's classroom (Ward 1987; Schlechty 1985). In addition, some induction projects include the development of *specific instructional skills* designed to increase the effectiveness of the new teacher. These might include *Improved Instruction* (Hunter 1973), *Building Classroom Discipline* (Charles 1985), cooperative learning, ESL techniques, or any number of other instructional approaches. Modeling, observation, and feedback may be specifically tied to these instructional goals.

A final potential role for support teachers is that of *assessment*. In a number of states, the assessment of new teachers prior to permanent certification has been legislated as a companion to the provision of new teacher support (Odell 1987). In some of these states, the consulting teacher is one of a team (often with an administrator and a university person) that observes and evaluates the beginning teacher. Other states

54

maintain this basic format but specifically designate the consultant as the one who helps the new teacher prepare a portfolio for evaluation or who presents this portfolio to the committee as the new teacher's advocate. Whatever form it takes, involvement of the consulting teacher in new teacher assessment dramatically changes the nature of the support relationship—no longer is it strictly confidential and nonevaluative. Consequently, this change affects decisions made in relation to the training and selection of, and incentives offered to teacher consultants (Odell 1987).

TRAINING

The basic decisions about support teacher training flow naturally from the definition of their role—whether it is basically orientation, psychological support, curricular or instructional advice, observation and feedback, modeling effective teaching techniques, facilitating specific instructional approaches, assessment, or a combination of these. Implicit in all of these potential roles is the assumption that the consulting teacher possesses good communication skills and can facilitate problem identification by the new teacher. These skills are particularly needed when providing psychological support and cannot be taken as givens. Their importance points to a need for training in *coaching* techniques. If support teachers are expected to provide orientation or curricular or instructional advice, training may be limited to distributing handbooks and resource lists or to encouraging consultants to share ideas among themselves.

An expectation of classroom observation and feedback suggests that coaching training incorporate elements of *clinical supervision* to enable consulting teachers to provide explicit and nonevaluative input to their partner (Kester and Marockie 1987). When observation, feedback, and modeling are designed to reinforce specific teaching strategies, the teacher consultant must receive *training in the specific methodologies as well as in coaching and observation processes*. Finally, if consulting teachers are also required to participate in beginning teacher assessment, training in the *assessment program to be implemented* is essential. In this instance, training is not simply advisable in order to increase support effectiveness, it is mandatory because decisions affecting the future of the novice are based on the results of the consultant's evaluation.

Once the purpose and content of consultant training has been established, procedural decisions must be made. A key procedural question is, *should training take place during the school day or on the teacher consultants' own time?* Training during the day has the advantage of maximizing teacher energy and making high levels of attendance most likely. On the negative side, released time is expensive and in some districts quality substitutes are difficult to find. In addition, many experienced teachers are reluctant to leave their classes frequently—an important consideration if released days are needed for modeling and observation as well as for training.

A second procedural question must be addressed if the induction program involves training in specific instructional approaches. The question here is *whether some aspects of the training should take place with both the new teacher and support teacher in attendance*. In such a design, the partners receive information about the new methodology together and practice it during the training. Then the support teachers model it in their own classrooms and later observe and provide feedback when the new teachers practice with their classes (Bernhardt 1988). Obviously, such a design is complicated to implement. However, it promotes a very consistent and focused program and contains all of the elements identified by Joyce and Showers (1980) as necessary for true changes in teacher behavior to take place.

INCENTIVES

As outlined in Table 1, induction programs where the support teacher's role is limited to orientation, psychological support, and advice require minimal training and may not require extensive incentives. On the other hand, programs featuring in-depth training and released time for modeling and observation may require greater incentives, particularly to sustain them over the long term.

As has already been alluded to, there are many disincentives to becoming a support teacher: the amount of personal time required, absences from one's own classes, and substitute problems. Fear of being paired with an unsuccessful beginning teacher, whose lack of success could be blamed on the teacher consultant, can also serve as a deterrent. And, in some school cultures, any attempt to differentiate oneself from other teachers can lead to resentment and peer isolation. What, then, can an induction program offer as inducements for the participation of experienced teachers? The most powerful incentive is one that can only be sought, not provided. This is a *commitment to the profession and a desire to play a role in its improvement*. Incentives that induction programs can offer include the *opportunity for professional growth* through the training sessions, *revitalization by a change in role* (from classroom teacher to consultant), *recognition*, a chance simply to get out of the classroom periodically, and an opportunity to *reduce their own profes-sional isolation*. These incentives can be heightened if becoming a consulting teacher is seen as a step toward becoming a mentor teacher, a curriculum specialist, or some other career-enhancing move. More tangible rewards include *university units, stipends, and reimbursements for professional materials* (Bernhardt 1988; Ward and Tikunoff 1988; Waters 1988). Each of these is potentially useful but can be problematic. University units are good only for consulting teachers who are not at the top of the salary schedule or who do not already have a master's degree. Stipends can be seen as compensation by teachers' associations and thus potentially subject to collective bargaining agreements. And reimbursements necessitate extensive paperwork for both the teacher consultant and the project (Ward and Tikunoff 1988). Another practical consideration is that small districts or districts with high teacher turnover must be careful to design their training and incentive programs so that experienced teachers are encouraged to serve as teacher consultants more than once (Bernhardt 1988). Once again, there is no one perfect incentive package and districts are left to weigh the various options in terms of their program resources and constraints.

SELECTION

The definition of the consulting teacher's role, along with the training required and incentives offered, lays the groundwork for the selection criteria and procedures. An orientation role calls for *experience at the site and in the district*. An expectation of psychological support necessitates *personal characteristics* such as warmth, empathy, listening skills, and an ability to instill trust and provide confidentiality. Ideally, there would also be an opportunity to provide some type of *personality fit* between the experienced teacher and the novice. The responsibility of offering curricular or instructional advice, modeling, providing observation and feedback, and facilitating the development of specific instructional skills all demand that the consultant be an *excellent and experienced teacher*. Optimally, such a support teacher would also be *closely matched* with the novice in terms of classroom proximity, grade level, subject, and special features such as being in a bilingual program or the same year-round track (Gray and Gray 1985). The teacher consultant roles of modeling and assessment require a special selection consideration—*willingness*. Some teachers are uncomfortable being observed. Many more are reticent to evaluate their peers. Such responsibilities, then, must be laid out clearly when consulting teachers are being recruited and selected.

An additional consideration in selection involves time. Effective teacher consultants must spend a significant amount of time with their new teachers. Not only must they have the *commitment* to make this time available, but they *cannot be overcommitted* with other school leadership or community activities. Often the best role models, and potentially the most committed, are also overcommitted.

Unfortunately, these ideal conditions are not always possible, particularly in small schools or schools receiving large numbers of new teachers. In such cases, judgments must be made. Even in the best of situations, where ample numbers of quality prospective support teachers can be found, a basic dilemma exists: the need for *careful selection to assure quality and match versus the need for timeliness*. The most stressful period for new teachers is often at the beginning of that first year (Martin-Newman 1988). Ideally, this is when the consultant should be most available for orientation and psychological support. The matching process is enhanced by new teacher input (to help ensure compatibility) and administrative participation (to generate program ownership and to gain a wider perspective on the ability and availability of prospective consultants). But given the chaotic nature of the first few weeks before and after the beginning of school and the late hiring of many new teachers, careful selection makes immediate pairing extremely difficult. Further complications arise if a selection panel of teachers is also used either because of the teachers' unique perspective to generate program support, or because of contractual agreements (when payment is involved). The complications just detailed are exacerbated when there is distrust between any of the parties involved.

One California school district's response to the tension between providing timely orientation support and careful consulting teacher selection has been to assign a district mentor from the State Mentor Teacher Program to each new teacher on hire. At this point, a general match (grade level, subject area, and section of town) is made. This provides orientation and rudimentary psychological support for the opening of school and allows time for a more careful selection of the permanent consulting teacher (Waters 1988).

CONCLUSION

Experienced teacher support is a potent element in the induction of beginning teachers. Through this partnership, new teachers can receive orientation, psychological support, instructional advice, and what can become a year-long individualized instructional development program.

Such support not only increases retention but also improves teaching performance (Huling-Austin 1988). Interestingly, it can also improve the classroom effectiveness of experienced teachers (Bernhardt 1988). However, these gains are not automatic. In order to realize the full potential of experienced teacher support, care must be taken so that the role expectations, training programs, incentive plans, and selection procedures are mutually reinforcing. Congruency is the key word in establishing the mutually reinforcing components for support teacher success. *Role expectations* must be clear and well-thought through so that teacher consultant support does indeed result in the desired outcomes of the program—be these increased new teacher effectiveness, psychological well-being, retention, or any other programmatic goal. *Selection criteria* must then be tailored to bring on board consulting teachers appropriate to the roles they are expected to fulfill. Once role expectations and selection criteria have been established, *training* to enable support teachers to meet these expectations can be designed. This training must be clearly focused and intense enough to allow support teachers to implement the specific induction model on their own without continual monitoring by project administrators. And finally, *incentives* for experienced teacher participation must be tied both to the demands of the support teacher role and to the values of the types of individuals likely to be selected. Important choices must be made in each arena—roles, training, incentives, and selection—to tailor a program that meets the unique needs and resources of each district. But the care taken in the planning stage can pay great dividends in the success of an induction program.

REFERENCES

Bernhardt, V. C. 1988. *Induction for the beginning teacher: Program evaluation results*. Chico, CA: California State University.

Charles, C. M. 1985. *Building classroom discipline*. New York: Longman, 87–100.

Gray, W. A., and Gray, M. M. 1985. Synthesis of research on mentoring beginning teachers. *Educational Leadership* 45 (3): 37–43.

Hoffman, J.; O'Neal, S.; and Paulissen, M. 1986. A study of state-mandated beginning teacher programs and their effects. In *Reality and reform in clinical teacher education*, ed. J. V. Hoffman and S. A. Edwards, 147–53. New York: Random House.

Huling-Austin, L. 1988. *A synthesis of research on teacher induction programs and practices*. Paper presented at the annual meeting of the American Educational Research Association, New Orleans.

Huling-Austin, L., and Murphy, S. C. 1987. *Assessing the impact of teacher induction programs: Implications for program development.* Paper presented at the annual meeting of the American Educational Research Association, Washington, DC. ERIC No. 283 779.

Huling-Austin, L.; Putman, S.; and Galvez-Hjornevik, C. 1985. *Model Teacher Induction Project study findings: Final report.* Austin: University of Texas, Research and Development Center for Teacher Education. ERIC No. ED 270 442.

Hunter, Madeline. 1973. *Improved instruction.* E. L. Segundo, CA: TIP Publications.

Joyce, B., and Showers, B. 1980. Improving inservice training: The messages of research. *Educational Leadership* (Feb.): 379-85.

Kester, R., and Marockie, M. 1987. Local induction programs. In *Teacher induction: A new beginning,* ed. D. M. Brooks. Reston, VA: Association of Teacher Educators.

Marso, R. N., and Pigge, F. L. 1986. *Beginning teachers: Expectation vs. realities.* Paper presented at the 41st annual meeting of the Association for Supervision and Curriculum Development, San Francisco.

Martin-Newman, D. 1988. *Internal evaluation.* Oakland-California State University, Hayward New Teacher Support Project.

Odell, S. J. 1987. *Teacher induction: Rationale and issues.* In *Teacher induction: A new beginning,* ed. D. M. Brooks, 73–76. Reston, VA: Association of Teacher Educators.

Schlechty, P. C. 1985. A framework for evaluating induction into teaching. *Journal of Teacher Education* 36 (1): 37–41.

Ward, B. 1987. State and district structures to support initial year of teaching programs. In *The first years of teaching: Background papers and a proposal,* ed. G. Griffin and S. Millies. Chicago: University of Illinois at Chicago in cooperation with Illinois State Board of Education.

Ward, B. A., and Tikunoff, W. J. *Implementation study: New teacher retention in inner-city schools project.* Los Alamitos, CA: Southwest Regional Laboratory.

Waters, L. B. 1988. *Third year proposal.* Oakland-California State University, Hayward New Teacher Support Project.

Wildman, T. M.; Niles, J. A.; Magliaro, S. G.; McLaughlin, R. A.; and Drill, L. G. 1987. *Virginia's colleague teacher project: Focus on beginning teachers' adaptation to teaching.* Paper presented at the annual meeting of the American Educational Research Association, Washington, DC.

6. INDEPENDENT ACTION: CASE STUDIES OF ITS ROLE IN BEGINNING TEACHERS' INDUCTION

by Carol P. Etheridge

Despite recommendations and efforts to provide beginning teachers support through the preparation/induction period (Huling-Austin and Murphy 1987; Barnes 1983), too many beginning teachers have problems applying their pedagogical learning in the real-life situation. They learn how to cope with the problems of teaching through on-the-job experience. Thus, each generation of teachers rediscovers the pedagogical wheel. Shulman (1987) called this situation "collective amnesia." It exists because the education profession lacks a case literature to provide the wisdom of practice.

Case reports are holistic data that "retain the meaningful characteristics of real-life events" (Yin 1984, p. 14). They can be an integral part of teacher preparation because case reports provide first-hand appreciation of, and experience with, the application of knowledge to practice (Christensen and Hansen 1987). Cases are a mirror and mechanism for more complete understanding of teacher thinking and action—for both professors and students of teaching. By reading and discussing cases, teacher education students begin to cumulatively acquire, combine, and reorder a set of experiences. This then allows them to discover and develop their own unique framework for approaching, understanding, and dealing with education problems before entering the real world of practice. Thus, they acquire working knowledge of school realities and realize that there are no recipes for teaching. For practicing teachers, cases become a catalyst to reexamine familiar frameworks or to develop new concepts and priorities regarding teaching.

As part of the formative evaluation of two teacher preparation programs,* a group of 31 beginning teachers were followed from the beginning of their preparation/induction programs into their second teaching year. Data were collected through participant observation in summer

---

*The project was sponsored by the Center of Excellence in Teacher Education, College of Education, Memphis State University.

coursework and in-depth interviews conducted throughout coursework, internships, and the first and second teaching years. In addition to interviewing the beginning teachers, principals, supervising teachers, and professors who worked with the beginning teachers were interviewed. From the detailed data collected, ten case studies were completed representing varied themes.

The three cases presented here illustrate independent action as it was exhibited by the beginning teachers. To simulate how the cases may be used in teacher preparation, ask yourself the following questions about each case:

1. How did the teacher exhibit independence?

2. What significant factors seemed to contribute to the teacher's chosen course of action?

3. What are the pros and cons of the teacher's actions?

4. What alternate actions might the teacher have taken?

CLARA

Thirty-four years old, married, with two preschool children, confidently capable, businesslike, self-directing, and committed to teaching well, Clara's watchwords might be , "If you aren't going to lead or follow, get out of the way." When entering the phased internship program, Clara held a bachelor's degree in humanities, a master's degree in mathematics, and the determination to teach. She embarked on a degree in education with embarrassment, but it was the only avenue to certification.

I want to be a teacher. I do not want to be an education dummy. I will be teaching and I will be teaching for a long time because I like to teach. But, I am going to go back (to the university) someday and get a real degree, a real content degree. Thousands get degrees in education.

Clara's third internship placement at Queensland Junior High, an urban school serving an integrated poor and working class population, helped her to discover and become comfortable with the teaching methods that she preferred. Her case is best told in her words.

Phased Internship

In the first two teaching placements, my teachers were very high-strung, very tense, almost antagonistic. They made abrasive statements. In phase three, the teacher was very relaxed in a situation where the students were not terrific. They were low-income Black kids and the potential existed for serious discipline problems, but she was relaxed, not tense and upset. She didn't hate the system, kids, or the school. She didn't hate what she was doing. I thought, "WOW, she's been teaching for 12, 18 years and still has feelings like that; there are people who really like teaching." Then I thought, "I can do that."

My teacher could change her mood according to what the kids needed. Some of her classes were very structured, some were not. She was comfortable being down with the kids; all the kids came around her in a circle and she sat in the middle. Other teachers wouldn't get close to the kids. They needed to have some kind of a fence but this teacher, my teacher, wasn't like that. I thought, "That's how I wanted to teach all along!" I realized that people can be successful at teaching this type of child by being human and I thought I could be human and be a successful teacher.

First Teaching Year

I was hired on an interim contract at Pine Valley Junior High. No one wants to teach here. The teachers are either beginning teachers with no choice, or the teachers have been here a long while and like it because there is no accountability. No one checks on them, no parents come around and ask about what is taught.

I teach five sections of eighth grade math—one preparation. Some are ahead of the others but basically they are all the same. I teach basic skills and go over and over them. These students don't plan ahead, so we take each day at a time. Even then, I divide the period and say that they have only 30 minutes left; they can deal with that. I tell them how many days are left in the six weeks, how many weeks are left in the semester.

I was evaluated several times this year. At first, they told me that I must teach from the curriculum guide. I quickly figured out that I couldn't teach those objectives because these students don't have good preparation. During the first month I was here, a supervisor asked why I wasn't teaching to the objectives in the guide. I told her that my students didn't know how to bring books to class and that was what we were working on. When they knew to do that, I would get around to teaching math. I don't use the curriculum guide at all. The principal is supportive; he says to do what the students need.

The first ten weeks were hell because I tried to be nice but firm. The kids ran over me. I sent kids to the office and they were sent back; I got no support for discipline. I took students to the vice principal and he didn't do anything. I figure that I am here to teach and the office is supposed to keep control, but they didn't do it, so I started reading and learned that the teacher can discipline her students as long as an administrator is present. So I bought a big paddle and beat the hell out of kids for three weeks. Every day I took a crowd of kids to the office and beat them. After three weeks of beating to shape them up, I got their attention and now I don't spank them.

I think a lot of my problems are racial. The administrator tells me not to touch any of the kids, white teachers cannot touch kids. I told him that nowhere in my contract does it say not to touch kids. I'll touch if I want.

A lot of my behavior has changed. I learned that yelling doesn't help and for some kids, spanking doesn't help. I tried calling parents but that was not effective either. So I do strange things, like the other day I threw an eraser at a boy to get his attention. I also tell them that if I have to fill out a conference report form, they'll get suspended. That works.

I am on the guidance committee, the Mr. and Miss Pine Valley committee, and the discipline committee. I also tutor kids after school. The principal requires nothing, we don't even have to make lesson plans. There are no demands. I'm looking out for myself so I'll be ready to move when there is an opening in a better school.

Mostly I have learned on my own what I need to survive. No support is available from the math department. The seventh grade math teacher is certified in science and she asks me for my answer sheets so that she can grade her tests. I have been evaluated by the system but I have no real idea how I am doing. I get no feedback from parents, administrators, etc., and I have no (standardized) test scores yet. I'm beginning to build my reputation and so far I think it is good.

Second Teaching Year

I was declared surplus in August and received a letter telling me that I was placed at Scott Junior High. I didn't want to teach at Scott but was told if I didn't like that placement I could quit. My math supervisor and teachers I knew in the system said that I would be OK at Scott, so I decided to take the job. I'm sorry I did. The students are not the reason. They have no background, no talent, no motivation, no supervision, and no money. But they have heart.

The administration is terrible; they let things slide and don't care about the kids. They don't consistently promote any expectations from students or teachers. For example, teachers are directed to fail no more than 30 percent of their students, so the teachers have calculated how many Fs they can give each six weeks. I have not done this. The first six weeks, 64 percent of my students failed and the second six weeks, 31 percent failed. I work to teach my students and I expect them to work in my classes. If they come to class with no books, that's OK. I have extra books. They come with no paper, that's OK. They can borrow some. No pencils—I sell them pencils. I make things available for kids to be successful. If students come to class, I can teach them but what I don't tolerate is them not working on the lesson. I realize this is necessary if they are to learn. I force mastery and give no extra credit; all my grading is criterion-based. They either learn it or they don't. When they ask for extra credit, I give them the last test they failed and tell them to take it home and work on it. If they need help, I help them. When they master the material, I give them credit, so no one fails if they learn the material.

Last year, I paddled kids. This year, no—the administration will not allow it. Last year, they told us that we weren't allowed to touch the Black kids, but I touched them anyway. I still touch them, pat them, hug them—and they touch me. I think it is good. I have to do what is right for me in the classroom.

I teach seventh and eight grade math. The kids in seventh grade look to take eighth grade math and in eighth grade, they are looking to take ninth grade math. Nobody expects anything of them and they don't expect anything of themselves, but I don't accept that. My students are being prepared for prealgebra and algebra. They are not dumb and I believe they can learn.

The principal evaluated me a while back; I had a good lesson on decimals. We didn't practice it the day before like other teachers do. I had 15 laminated menus from the Nam King restaurant. Students worked in groups role playing, with some being waiters and taking orders, and others ordering from the menus. These kids never eat out anywhere, let alone at a Chinese restaurant, so I thought maybe it was a small chance for them to see how the rest of the world lives. They looked at the menus and read the dinners and grimaced and made noises, but they got into the lesson. I modeled what they were to do and they all did the lesson—they did what they were supposed to do, calculating totals and figuring change.

One time an incident occurred when some students, who were basically thugs and emotionally disturbed, threatened me. Several boys and girls were late to class. The girls entered the room and mumbled something about being late and they went to their seats. No big deal. Then the boys came to the door yelling profanities, calling me a bitch, and saying that I could not tell them what to do. Immediately, I shut the door and would not let them into the room. They started kicking and banging on the door and yelling. I called to the office for assistance. Classes changed and the boys left but no one ever came to help.

I found a way to handle behavior problems by taking several layers of action. First, I talk to the student. If that doesn't work, I call for a parent conference; if parents don't come in within three days, the student is put on board suspension. That is such a hassle for the parents that they come for the conference and usually the conference gets action. I find that simply calling parents does not work; they have to come to school and talk face to face. Conferences create opportunity for parents to see how students behave in the halls and in the classrooms. Sometimes they are surprised and embarrassed; they don't want their children to misbehave. Parents tell their children that if they can't do anything else, they can behave in class. I find parents to be very supportive; some even thank me for contacting them.

If conferencing doesn't work, I talk with the guidance people. Finally, if I still don't get results, I do a psychological referral. The counseling department must respond to the psychological referral within one week and usually, the student is removed. The conference-referral combination works when the administration enforces the rules. To ensure that happens, I have to double- and triple-check on the administration—it gets tiring.

I continue to volunteer a lot. I'm on the guidance committee and discipline committee and I work with the crafts club. I conducted a workshop at the community college on using nontraditional methods in traditional classrooms, and I'm on the next in-service roster to do a workshop for the system's math teachers. I am also active in the math teacher's associations; it provides the intellectual stimulation I need.

I don't know if I can do this (teach in this type of setting) much longer. I have to be very active and alert at all times, moving around the classroom and attending to the students. Teaching this type of student means always being psychologically up. It is very wearing. I have to admit that my preparation program has served me better than I originally thought; I may come back for a doctorate in education.

SAM

Sam, ex-navy, held a bachelor's degree in physics and math and a master's degree in physics. Independent, personable, intelligent, he was in love with his subject field. A 29-year-old bachelor when entering the program, he married prior to completion of the internship. Various professors encouraged him to pursue an advanced physics degree but he opted for teacher certification. Because he had tutoring experience, Sam felt he understood the components of physics that cause problems for students, thus, he was confident that he would be an excellent physics teacher.

Sam believed that the teaching profession needed reform, especially in the quality of instruction provided to high school science students. Arts and sciences graduates, he was convinced, were the answer to education's instructional and status problems and that was his justification for being a teacher. "The lesser qualified students go to the college of education.... They need arts and sciences people to straighten things out, which is why they set up this teacher preparation program for folks like us." To his surprise, Sam found education faculty to be capable, thus, early in the program he decided that he would learn useful knowledge and skills.

Immersion Internship

Eagerly, Sam engaged the internship with confidence. Knowing he would be a physics teacher at LaGrange, a suburban school with an academic optional program, Sam went to school, sorted the lab equipment, and ordered supplies before school and the internship began. Soon he persuaded the principal to establish a physics section for advanced students, which he taught in addition to his internship assignment. He also declared the physics textbook to be "lousy" and requested new texts. No money was available, so he devised his own curriculum.

Sam never "talked or anything" with his cooperating teacher, whose primary area was chemistry, but did "... help her with two labs. I let her know we ordered a laser and told her some labs she could do with it." He adopted another chemistry teacher with whom he established a close relationship and he worked closely with a physics professor from whom he had taken coursework. Together they designed, and Sam taught, a curriculum for the advanced physics class.

Sam poured his energies into teaching physics. He tutored and located resource materials and people during his planning periods and after school; he graded papers and encouraged students to call him for assistance in the evenings. By completion of Sam's internship year, projections were that the next year's physics enrollment would more than double, with at least 50 students taking calculus-based physics. Sam was offered a teaching position at LaGrange, which he gladly accepted.

First Teaching Year

Initially, Sam's assignment included one chemistry section, four large physics sections, homeroom, and a planning period. He disliked large classes, so he negotiated away the planning period and homeroom for an additional physics class, thus, "trig physics" and "calc physics" could be offered.

In physics, he described himself as demanding but relaxed. Physics students were allowed to drink cokes and talk because they cleaned up after themselves and talked about physics problems. He tutored and worked with small groups less than in the previous year because he had no planning period, a new baby at home, and he noticed that students did not study the material until at the study session. Instead of tutoring individuals, Sam worked his students in groups. He reported, "It's hard to do because they don't like working in groups. I make them do it and as a result, I notice that at lunch they get together and talk about physics with students from various physics classes."

Chemistry was different. Although he was certified in chemistry, he had not dealt with it for eight years; thus he was uncomfortable with the content. He planned no chemistry labs because he felt too inexperienced and was reticent to risk endangering students by planning improperly designed labs. Demonstrations replaced labs and no assistance was sought for this problem. Chemistry students were mostly sophomores and less serious students, so they were not allowed to drink cokes or talk. "They talk about their social lives instead of chemistry." Because of behavior problems encountered in chemistry class, Sam established rules of behavior and began treating his students like "junior high school kids," telling them what to do, when, and how.

Initially, he thought the chemistry students' learning problems stemmed from their desire to memorize. They wanted to be told to memorize a formula and when to apply it, but Sam encouraged them to search for regularities. After semester break, he decided he was pampering his chemistry students. "I got mean and nasty and made them work. The harder it got, the more they liked it." He abandoned the chemistry text and wrote his own chemistry curriculum. Throughout the rest of the academic year, Sam constantly adjusted the chemistry and physics curriculums and planned for the following year.

He noticed that biology and chemistry were budgeted the bulk of the school's science funds because of higher student enrollment. He also recognized that, "There is pressure from (standardized) tests to teach a set amount of material and content." But he decided, "I don't care if I have the volume of content. I must teach the course so a higher percentage of students will want to take physics." He then linked with the physical science teachers by teaching them labs and demonstrations for their classes and offering to order equipment. They gladly accepted the assistance as most were trained in chemistry. The linkage created "the largest unit in the sciences," so the following year equipment money was divided evenly between life sciences and physical sciences. "I can order equipment and materials for physical science that can be used in physics, so I will have the equipment necessary for my labs."

JOELLE

Capable, quiet Joelle, 29 years old, held an engineering degree but never worked as an engineer because, "I was the first in my family to earn a college degree and I had no contacts to help me get a job. I turned down chances for summer internships with industry because I wanted to finish my degree. Now I realize those internships were opportunities for entry into the job market that is closed to me now." Joelle supported herself by tutoring high school and college students until a friend suggested she investigate a fifth-year teacher certification program. Joelle applied and was admitted even though, "I knew that many people look down on teaching ... but I viewed teachers as having responsibility equal to doctors, lawyers, and engineers."

Immersion Internship

Her internship placement, like Sam's, was at LaGrange High School. Joelle taught one honors chemistry and two regular chemistry classes. The internship was stressful because she was isolated from the other science teachers and from sources of assistance. "I'm in a building by myself. All the science teachers are in another building. . . . . Nobody told me about how other teachers wouldn't have time to help me, or that I would be given tasks with no direction, or that the secretary wouldn't have time to explain." In addition, she and her cooperating teacher did not communicate well and she felt he caused her to look incompetent, as her description implies:

He told me, "Don't do a lab." I had to give labs but he would say, "No, don't do a lab yet." He would do a lab and I would find out from the students. One day he did a lab and told me to do the lab with my class on that day too—no preparation, nothing written down for me to see. I took my class and they were confused and so was I. Of course, it looked like I had no idea what I was doing. I decided I would do labs without him.

But chemicals were not available for her labs. "Out of desperation I went to my high school chemistry teacher who helped me. He didn't have the chemicals I needed but he told me to make a list and put in a rush order for everything I needed." She also found support and advice in the faculty lounge from the school librarian, a history teacher, and the typing teacher. Additionally, she accessed a university professor who was unrelated to her program. Joelle persevered. Despite her disappointing internship, she applied for a position in the school system where she interned.

First Teaching Year

She accepted a position teaching five sections of chemistry at LaGrange. She was pleased to be back because she knew the school's procedural nuances and some of the faculty. Additionally, she felt teachers had more professional status at LaGrange than at other less esteemed schools.

As in her internship, Joelle continued teaching in a building removed from the other science teachers and had minimal contact with them. "I did it myself," she said, "So now I don't need people to help me." Her ex-teacher, as department chairman, continued to discourage her from doing labs. "He thinks the lab is his, not ours. He does not want me to do labs for three days out of the week but it doesn't matter that he does labs for three days."

Joelle taught the same basic material to her standard and honors classes although the standard class, she reported, did more problem solving because of the book they used. Her teaching mode was direct instruction, primarily lecture coupled with blackboard or overhead projector to illustrate or write important points. Throughout the teaching year, she had behavior problems in labs. Her labs came directly from the textbook which, after teaching them, she realized were too long and complicated for her students. She planned to adjust.

Second Teaching Year

In the same school, with the same teaching assignment, Joelle continued to like the students and felt they reciprocated. When her students did poorly, she asked them why and revised her instruction or determined whether students needed more study time, "I talk to them and find out why . . . If their reason is legitimate, I let them retake the test. Sometimes they tell me they can't understand the way I phrase something or they give other constructive criticism. That helps me."

From the beginning, Joelle expressed displeasure with the record-keeping, paperwork, long working hours, and poor relationship with her chemistry colleagues. This year, however, she devised ways to ease her life. First, she improved her working relationship with chemistry colleagues by "complimenting everyone's teaching" and by giving new teachers tips about organizing homeroom and doing labs. She also reconciled the hostility with her ex-teacher. "I got rid of him as department chairman. It hurt his feelings but I nominated someone else. He is a lonely man and likes to talk, so I praise him a lot and we get along OK now."

Joelle tried to organize the chemistry teachers to compile one master set of lesson plans that all could use and to coordinate chemistry labs. It never came to fruition, so she decided to go it alone and shared with no one unless asked. For example, she determined that last year's lab problems stemmed from labs that were too long and complicated for the equipment available at LaGrange. Therefore, she designed simpler, shorter labs that were more successful; she shared them with other teachers who asked about them. She located a lab book containing short labs and the principal agreed to buy one complete set. "He wants all the chemistry teachers to use it. I'm looking out for myself."

With interpersonal and technical teaching problems resolved, Joelle worked on decreasing the time spent on paperwork and class preparations. Her daily planning period was inadequate for planning classes and labs, doing lab setups, and grading papers, so she eliminated some paper-grading time by giving objective tests and machine-scoring them.

To keep from doing schoolwork at home on weekends, she devised several strategies. First, she taught for 25 or 30 minutes during each class period. "I give them an assignment and I work on the next day's lesson. This way I get two hours each day for planning." Then she planned independent reading or writing activities for her students so that she could "stop teaching on Mondays and Fridays." On Monday, she planned for the rest of the week; on Friday, she did recordkeeping and paper grading. Thus, she eliminated considerable weekend work. To shorten time spent on lab preparations and recordkeeping, she trained two students to set up labs and enter grades on the computer. Other efforts to create time for herself included engaging in no extracurricular responsibilities, except for minor ones required of all faculty such as attending occasional athletic events. When possible, she skipped staff development sessions because she felt her time was better spent on planning activities.

DISCUSSION

The teacher preparation programs through which Clara, Sam, and Joelle were prepared emphasized independence, reflection, innovation, sensitivity to students, and diverse use of teaching strategies. It is impossible to generalize to the broader population from the experiences of these three individuals, but patterns emerge that shed light on what happens to neophyte teachers who were prepared as these were. They began, if not with praise for their preparation, with the willingness to learn and the certainty that they would succeed and make a difference in the world of schools. They entered their workplaces with the ability to take independent action, a sense of confidence, an attitude of experimentation, and the willingness to become leaders in the field, or at least shining lights among the humdrum of the teaching population.

These beginning teachers were independent thinking and acting individuals, but their internship experiences either facilitated or forced further independence. Both Clara and Sam's internship experiences facilitated their independent actions. Clara ultimately worked with a cooperating teacher whom she admired. The teacher was the mechanism through which Clara clarified her concept of how teaching should occur for her, and then reinforced that concept. Though there was little evidence of Clara's independent actions in the internship, the experience seemed to enable Clara, as a certified teacher, to maintain a positive outlook, act independently, and justify her practices to others, even in the face of bad situations and criticism from supervisors. She was able to act, based on her students' needs and her own survival needs, and to take actions that enhanced both.

Sam's internship experience facilitated his independent action in a different way. As sometimes happens when induction field experiences are designed to provide mechanisms for support and instruction, they do not always work as planned. Sam's arranged support system did not materialize, but he developed relationships with two individuals who effectively replaced the planned support. With the support system, Sam's independence and innovations were nurtured, giving him greater confidence. Thus, as a certified teacher, he continued to be innovative and positive as he searched for teaching strategies that would enhance his students' learning. Both he and Clara, through their independent actions, were able to be innovative and implement teaching practices that were pedagogically sound, while making their own teaching lives easier.

In Joelle's case, the induction field experience forced her to be more independent than she desired to be at the time. Joelle and her cooperating teacher did not interact well, and she was isolated from other science teachers. Thus, her opportunity to establish an alternative strong support system was diminished and she made do with casual support from a group of teachers outside her subject field. She was forced to act independently in establishing her teaching strategies as an intern. Her independent actions seemed polarized from her cooperating teacher, defensive, and focused on her own survival rather than on her professional growth and her students' learning. Because she struggled to survive alone, her view of teaching became jaded even before she was certified. Then, as a first-year teacher, she survived by relying on textbooks to structure her curriculum and teaching strategies, seemingly focused on survival. As a second-year teacher, she focused on the negatives of her teaching situation and on her needs. This led to failed attempts to organize cooperative planning with colleagues and to implementing teaching practices that were not always in the best interest of her students.

Clara and Sam might reasonably be expected to become positive forces affecting the profession and students, but Joelle's path appears bound either for leaving the profession or for further refining of her survival strategies at the expense of her students. It seems clear that independent action enabled these beginners to survive. Independence alone did not produce actions that had the potential to favorably affect the schools and/or profession. But support during the internship induction experiences that nurtured the learner and allowed and encouraged independent and innovative action seemed to build the confidence necessary to take independent actions that could have a favorable impact on students, schools, and the profession.

REFERENCES

Barnes, S. 1983. Induction programs: Reports from three sites. In *Proceedings of a national conference on the first years of teaching,* ed. G. A. Griffin and H. Hukill, 97–106. Austin, TX: Research and Development Center for Teacher Education, University of Texas at Austin.

Christensen, C. R., and Hansen, A. J. 1987. *Teaching and the case method.* Boston: Harvard Business School.

Huling-Austin, L., and Murphy, S. C. 1987. *Assessing the impact of teacher induction programs: Implications for program development.* Paper presented at the annual meeting of the American Educational Research Association, Washington, DC.

Shulman, L. 1987. *A vision for teacher education.* Keynote address, Houston, TX: Association of Teacher Educators.

Yin, R. K. 1984. *Case study research: Design and methods.* Beverly Hills: Sage.

7. MULTIPLE SUPPORT: A PROMISING STRATEGY FOR EFFECTIVE TEACHER INDUCTION

by Marvin A. Henry

The first year of teaching has long been recognized as a difficult, if not *the* most difficult, year for teachers. Ironically, this usually is the time when support from universities is withdrawn and public school assistance is either minimal or perceived as evaluation. The entry year is further complicated by the fact that first-year assignments are often the most difficult ones that teachers face. It is not unusual for new teachers to be assigned low-ability classes, to have several preparations, to be moved to different rooms during the day, and to have a heavy extracurricular load. It is small wonder that the dropout statistics of young teachers are as much as 50 percent during the first five yars of teaching (Howey and Zimpher 1987). While other professions are prone to provide a supervised induction period, teachers have been left alone to solve their entry problems.

THE NEED FOR SUCCESSFUL INDUCTION

If the profession is to make progress in retaining teachers, it must devise successful programs that will reverse the high dropout and burnout rate. Beginning teachers are not yet ready to be full-fledged teachers regardless of the preservice program they go through (Ward 1987). When adequate support is unavailable, teachers tend to leave. Unfortunately, these who leave first are more likely to be the most academically talented individuals (Lyson and Falk 1984; Mark and Anderson 1985; Schlechty and Vance 1983). To make matters worse, for the large majority of those who remain, their teaching effectiveness wanes considerably after five years, and more substantial declines are evident after ten years (Rosenholtz 1987). These problems may be superficially addressed by such changes as higher academic standards, competency examinations, and extrinsic motivational techniques. But close examination of the conditions of teaching lead to the conclusion that a more positive approach is needed to retain teachers and improve the quality of their work.

After study of the relationship between characteristics of teacher education candidates and their attitudes, concerns, anxieties, and confidence level during teacher preparation, Pigge and Marso (1987) strongly recommended an induction program that would provide support for new teachers. Noticing that student teaching is strengthened through a support system, they speculate that it would seem likely that the first-year teacher would also benefit from similar help. This observation has been strengthened by data from Rossetto and Grosenick (1987), who studied the effects of collaborative teacher education, an induction program at the University of Oregon that has been in place since 1963. Their conclusion was that a cooperative induction program can be a positive mechanism for teacher education.

Although the data present a convincing case for cooperative, or multiple, support for beginning teachers, the type of support given will make all the difference in whether it helps to produce effective beginning teachers. Good support focuses on the daily problems that young teachers are facing and avoids linking supervision with evaluation. Literature shows that mentor support and peer support are quite helpful in successful induction (Hoffman and Defino 1986; Zeichner 1986; Cornett 1985; Edwards, 1984).

TYPES OF SUPPORT

Three types of support seem to offer the most promise for developing a model that will work: mentor support, peer support, and university support. Each approaches induction in a way that no other can. If any part of the triad is omitted, programs and beginning teachers may not succeed. But as noted above, each must be provided at a level of quality to be effective.

Mentor support is the most typical and perhaps most critical component of teacher induction. A mentor should be selected who is highly respected and has demonstrated a level of excellence in teaching. The mentor should be a model of the standards the profession is attempting to achieve. It is not enough to be a good teacher; a mentor needs time to work with a beginning teacher and may need to develop supervisory skills. A successful mentor must have human relations skills and conference skills as well as the ability to analyze teaching and provide feedback. The buddy system has operated for many years with varying degrees of success. A competent mentor will have duties more specifically ascribed and be more prepared to provide formative supervision.

Peer support offers the opportunity for those with similar experiences to share problems and ideas and to generate solutions. For these reasons, perhaps, peer support is popular among beginning teachers. Peer interaction, however, is not necessarily peer support. First, in order for real peer support to exist, a procedure must be in place that systematically gets beginning teachers together. This will likely transcend school district boundaries because many systems are presently adding a minimum number of new teachers to their faculties each year. Second, peers will need to be prepared to interact with each other with trust and empathy. Third, an agenda must be determined and a procedure developed that will allow for productive dialogue rather than merely sharing of experiences.

University supervision is emerging as another support base and complements peer and mentor assistance. This third dimension offers a variety of possibilities for improving the quality of the first-year experience and links teacher education to the initial performance of a teacher. Colleges and universities must be involved in the continuation process of teacher education for their own credibility as well as for the needs of the public schools and beginning teachers.

Howey and Zimpher (1987) identified eight activities in which institutions of higher education should engage in concert with the school to contribute to a more ideal focus of assistance to beginning teachers:

1. Assisting in the identification of problems and issues attendant to entry-year assistance and the development of sound policies.
2. Communicating realistic standards of performance.
3. Clarifying and establishing realistic ongoing working relationships between public schools and universities.
4. Providing direct services in the way of continuing education to beginning teachers.
5. Providing a variety of services to mentors.
6. Helping to establish conditions that allow for more clinical, reflective, and inquiry-oriented approaches to teaching.
7. Providing a model for induction activities that incorporates knowledge of classroom observation procedures.
8. Providing direction for needed research in how best to proceed with providing assistance and enabling beginning teachers to better learn how to teach on the job.

In addition to these activities, it is evident on the part of those who have had experience in teacher induction that there is benefit in having a support person who is not responsible to the governance of the school.

This enables a supervisor from a teacher eduction institution to be more candid and to be free from any intricacies and subtleties that may exist in a school setting. Furthermore, a university supervisor should be able to bring expertise and perspective on induction that may not exist in a given school district.

Pigge and Marso (1987) suggested that the supervisory triad, which has served student teaching so successfully, should be continued into the first year of teaching. This is a reasonable conclusion, but such supervision must be maintained at a level that offers the possibility of success in support for and retention of new teachers.

A MODEL FOR MULTIPLE SUPPORT

The notion that a triad of support from mentors, peers, and university supervisors would be effective was tested at Indiana State University in 1986 involving 20 first-year teachers in 15 different schools. The premise of the program was that integrated support would improve the quality of first-year teaching and possibly reduce teacher dropout because each one could make a contribution that was not possible by the other. Project CREDIT (Certification Renewal Experiences Designed to Improve Teaching) was initiated as a pilot program to test the theory and possibly to develop a model that could be incorporated into an ongoing program.

Public-school mentors were selected who were considered to be outstanding teachers and who would devote extra time to the supervision of the first-year teachers, called interns, in the project. Mentors were located in the same buildings as their interns and were involved with them daily, acting as role models and providing formative growth experiences. Approximately half worked with teachers in the same subject areas. Their responsibilities were to provide orientation, to help with problems, to assist in planning, to consult in subject-matter selection, and to help the new teacher understand the school culture. The mentors served solely as support persons and were not involved in the formal evaluation of the teachers.

Peer support came in two different ways. The most popular method was a monthly seminar, which was held in an informal setting where the interns could interact and talk about common experiences and problems. University personnel were available for participation and usually provided elaboration on a topic that might be of specific concern. Monthly meeting topics included discipline, methodology, testing and evaluating, handling stress, and human relations. A monthly newsletter containing teaching tips and ideas was published and distributed to the interns. The articles contained informative professional topics but also had features that would help to develop common interests in the group.

University support was provided through assistance from professors who were skilled in the supervision of field experiences. They made monthly site visits, observed classes, and consulted with the interns, mentors, and building administrators. Other university personnel were available to provide consultant services as needed. Their involvement was instrumental in developing the peer support.

The evaluation of Project CREDIT showed that the program was successful in intercepting declines in teaching attitudes. The participants in the program completed the year with significantly healthier attitudes and perceptions about teaching than did a similar group of beginning teachers who did not have multiple support. In addition, CREDIT interns excelled significantly over the control group in the ability to use mastery learning, motivation, higher order questions, critical thinking skills, awareness of curriculum guides, and communication with parents and the community. The results indicated that interns with multiple support were better able to cope with teaching variables than the control group on 88 of the 98 factors studied.

Mentor teachers and university supervisors were found to complement each other in the kinds of support that they were able to give to interns. Mentors assisted interns in understanding problems peculiar to the school, and university supervisors provided a surprising amount of personal and professional assistance that helped the beginner overcome problems generically associated with the first year of teaching.

The major finding was in the area of teacher retention. A follow-up study revealed that all 20 teachers in the program remained in teaching for a second year. This result stands in sharp contrast to normal dropout figures reported widely in the profession. The results seem to indicate that a multiple support program may be an effective way to retain teachers.

Project CREDIT is now in its third year and in 1988, was selected as the Association of Teacher Educators' Distinguished Program in Teacher Education. The results have been encouraging, although some of the barriers that inevitably surface in cooperative programs have to be addressed.

SUMMARY

One of the major problems in the emerging intern programs may be that their focus may tend to be too narrow when assistance is limited to a mentor who may or may not be trained for the position or have time released to perform the supervisory responsibilities. A mentor must be a good teacher, but she/he must also be a good coach who understands instructional supervision and must have the time to perform the necessary responsibilities needed for mentoring a new teacher. Most important, perhaps, is the fact that mentoring alone may not produce a complete induction experience. Peer support is needed to provide the opportunity for colleagues to learn from each other, but that learning must be structured in such a way that growth occurs. University personnel are necessary to facilitate peer interaction, to encourage mentors and first-year teachers, to provide a more comprehensive perspective on teacher development, and to be available as an external person who can use that vantage point to solve problems.

The experience of Project CREDIT seems to indicate that the three key elements of mentor, peer, and university support are necessary. The evaluation results of a pilot program support the contention that a well-structured support program can improve the teaching skills of first-year teachers as well as help to retain teachers in the profession. Finally, the program results seem to indicate that multiple support effectively extends teacher education into the first year of teaching, with responsibility being accepted by teacher education institutions as well as public schools.

REFERENCES

Brooks, Douglas. 1987. *Teacher induction. A new beginning.* Reston, VA: Association of Teacher Educators.

Cornett, L. M. 1985. Trends and emerging issues in career ladder plans. *Educational Leadership* 43 (3):6–10.

Edwards, S. A. 1984. *Local implementation of teacher induction programs.* Report No. 9059. Austin, TX: Research and Development Center for Teacher Education, University of Texas at Austin.

Griffin, Gary A., and Millies, Suzanne, eds. 1987. *The first years of teaching.* Chicago: University of Illinois at Chicago.

Hegler, Kay, and Dudley, Richard. 1987. Beginning teacher induction: A progress report. *Journal of Teacher Education* 38 (1): 53–56.

Hoffman, J. V., and Defino, M. E. 1986. *State and school district intentions and the implementation of new teacher programs.* Paper presented at the annual meeting of the American Educational Research Association, Chicago.

Howey, Kenneth R., and Zimpher, Nancy L. 1987. The role of higher education in initial year of teaching programs. In *The first years of teaching,* ed. G. A. Griffin and S. Millies. Chicago: University of Illinois at Chicago.

Lasley, Tom, ed. 1986. Teacher induction programs and research. *Journal of Teacher Education* 37 (1): 2–41.

Lyson, T. A., and Falk, W. 1984. Recruitment to school teaching: The relationship between high school plans and early adult attainments. *American Educational Research Journal* 21: 181–93.

Mark, J. H., and Anderson, B. D. 1985. Teacher survival rates in St. Louis, 1969–1982. *American Education Research Journal* 22: 413–21.

Pigge, Fred L., and Marso, R. N. 1987. Relationships between student characteristics and changes in attitutdes, concerns, anxieties, and confidence about teaching during teacher preparation. *Journal of Educational Research* 81 (2); 109–15.

Rosenholtz, Susan J. 1987. Workplace conditions of teacher quality and commitment: Implications for the design of teacher induction. In *The first years of teaching,* ed. G. A. Griffin and S. Millies. Chicago: University of Illinois at Chicago.

Rossetto, Celeste R., and Grosenick, Judith K. 1987. Effects of collaborative teacher education: Follow-up of graduates of a teacher induction program. *Journal of Teacher Education* 38 (2): 52–56.

Ryan, Kevin. 1986. *The induction of new teachers.* Bloomington, IN: Phi Delta Kappa.

Schlechty, P. C., and Vance, V. 1983. Recruitment, selection, and retention: The shape of the teaching force. *Elementary School Journal* 83: 469–87.

Ward, B. A. 1986. The policy and decision-making contexts of reform in clinical teacher education. In *Reality and reform in clinical teacher education,* ed. J. V. Hoffman and S. A. Edwards. New York: Random House.

————. 1987. State and district structures to support initial year of teaching programs. In *The first years of teaching,* ed. G. A. Griffin and S. Millies. Chicago: University of Illinois at Chicago.

Zeichner, K. M. 1986. Social and ethical dimensions of reform in teacher education. In *Reality and reform in teacher education,* ed. J. V. Hoffman and S. A. Edwards. New York: Random House.

8. BEGINNING TEACHERS: SINK OR SWIM?*

by Leonard J. Varah, Warren S. Theune, and Linda Parker

Teacher induction was initiated by the Wisconsin Improvement Program in 1971 and implemented in 1974 by University of Wisconsin-Whitewater. From 1974-84, the University experimented and developed a program to provide assistance and support for first-year teachers. Experimentation in all areas of elementary, secondary, and special education established that a coordinated induction program was an effective way to develop excellent staff and to retain the new members of the profession. As a result, the Teacher Induction Program received recognition from the university, the Department of Public Instruction, and the local schools. During the 1984-85 academic year, twelve inductees from six school districts participated in the program, and in 1985–86, twenty-one inductees from ten school districts are participating. The twenty-one inductees are receiving support and assistance from twenty-one mentor teachers, fourteen local administrators, and twelve University faculty.

Frequently cited problems of beginning teachers are discipline, isolation, evaluation of student work, and use of appropriate materials. The research has been conducted by Ryan (1970), Lortie (1975), Elias, Fisher, and Simon (1980), Veenman (1984), and others. Houston et al. (1979) reported research examining the problems and concerns of beginning teachers at selected times immediately preceding and during the first year of teaching. The researchers found that beginning teacher concerns focused on discipline methods, administrative approval, and communication in the school social setting.

Ryan et al. (1980) identified several areas of difficulty for first-year teachers. These areas include personal life adjustment, teachers' expectations and perceptions of teaching, the strains of daily interactions, and the teaching assignment itself. The researchers concluded that these difficulties lead to intense strain, which, in turn, leads to fatigue, depression and, subsequently, for many, exit from the profession.

Other studies have revealed the major concerns of beginning teachers

---

*This chapter is reprinted with permission from *Journal of Teacher Education*, January-February 1986, pp. 30–34. © 1986, American Association of Colleges of Teacher Education.

to be those of discipline and classroom management (Dropkin and Taylor, 1963; Grant and Zeichner 1981). In addition, discipline has been identified in two major reviews of the literature as the problem most frequently experienced by beginning teachers (Elias, Fisher, and Simon 1980; Veenman, 1984). Ryan (1974) concluded that "there is probably no single thing that causes beginning teachers more trouble and more anxiety than discipline problems" (p.11).

Veenman (1984) reviewed 91 studies and found that, in addition to discipline, the highest ranking problem areas were motivating students, dealing with individual differences, assessing students, dealing with heavy teaching loads and insufficient preparation time, developing relationships with colleagues, planning lessons, and preparing for the school day. Elias, Fisher, and Simon (1980) reported additional problems of finding and using appropriate materials, evaluating student work, and coping with a sense of isolation and insecurity.

Veenman (1984) observed that "there is remarkable homogeneity in the conclusions of the cited studies" (p. 166). He concluded that the more problems that a beginning teacher encountered, the more likely he or she was to leave teaching. In *Biting the Apple*, Ryan et al. (1980) stated, "Many of us who have studied what happens to first-year teachers believe that events during this initial year contribute to the gap between what they [beginning teachers] were capable of becoming and what they have, in fact, become" (p. 4).

Houston (1979) stated: "Teacher training institutions may never be able to prepare beginning teachers adequately unless pre-service teachers are provided opportunity to experience fully the responsibilities of teaching" (p. 19). Bush (1983) argued that new teachers develop a survival mentality and, that they have to learn to swim very quickly or sink. Dillon-Peterson (1982) stated that the first year of teaching is the most crucial period in a teacher's career. Sandefur (1982) observed that lack of appropriate induction is the major cause of teachers' leaving the profession during the first three years of teaching. The 1984 Wisconsin Department of Public Instruction Task Force Report on Teaching and Teacher Education indicated that (a) the most academically able teachers tend to be the first to leave education and are doing so in increasing numbers, and that (b) approximately 50 percent of those who take jobs as teachers leave the teaching profession within five years.

Houston (1979) made the following recommendation:

Teacher preparation programs must consider the provision of a year of internship as an imperative for adequately training teachers. It has been recommended by the AACTE Bicentennial Commission on Education for the Profession of Teaching that the internship in teacher education be defined as a minimum of one year of supervised employment and that it be made an integral part of all teacher preparation programs. (p. 20)

In attempting to meet this need to support and assist first-year teachers, the College of Education at the University of Wisconsin-Whitewater, in partnership with the Wisconsin Improvement Program and local schools, developed a Teacher Induction Program.

Induction has been described in many ways. According to Schlechty (1985), the purpose of induction is "to develop in new members of an occupation those skills, forms of knowledge, attitudes and values that are necessary to effectively carry out their occupational roles" (p.37). Tisher (1982) defined induction as assisting new teachers to be professionally competent. McDonald (1980b) defined induction as encompassing the mastery of two tasks—effective use of the skills of teaching and adapting to the social system of the school.

Eye (1956) defined induction as assisting teachers in adjusting to a new teaching environment. He explained that induction encompasses all activities, efforts, and experiences that are designed to assist newcomers to adapt satisfactorily to the new work and new situation. Eye asserted that the induction period begins as early as "the decision is made by the employing agent and the employed person to enter into a contractual relationship" (p. 68).

The University of Wisconsin-Whitewater Teacher Induction Program is intended to meet the needs of recently graduated and certified teaching candidates who have been hired as first-year teachers. School districts, cooperating with the university and supporting the idea of a planned program of guidance and support for beginners, encourage program participation by all first-year teachers employed. The goals of the program are listed in Figure 1. The statement of goals is followed by a description of the structure of the program.

PROGRAM DESCRIPTION

When the first-year teacher signs a contract in a participating school, the Induction Support Team is formed immediately. This team consists of a representative from the school's central administration, a mentor teacher, and a university consultant.

The representative from the central administration is an integral part of the planning unit but is not a part of the evaluation team that is to

Figure 1
Teacher Induction Program Goals

---

1. To provide a planned first-year teaching experience that makes possible a broad variety of professional learning experiences.
2. To reach a level of professional skill and judgment that characterize a well-qualified career teacher.
3. To raise professional competency to a level distinctly above that of the beginning teacher holding a bachelor's degree.
4. To re-examine numerous teaching techniques and instructional strategies and to experience others.
5. To develop extensive professional understanding and familiarity within the inductee's scope of certification.
6. To synthesize various learning theories and to study their application to different types of teaching and learning situations.
7. To develop an individual teaching style based on broad observation, discussion, and consultation.

---

determine the retention or dismissal of the new teacher. A mentor teacher is a teacher in the unit school teaching in the same subject area and at the same grade level as the inductee. The university consultant is a specialist in the teaching methodology of the subject and the grade level of the inductee.

Because the mentor is the key person who works with the first-year teacher, careful selection of a qualified person is crucial. Mentors are not appointed. A teacher must want to be a mentor. Two primary qualifications for the position are a dedication to teaching and a willingness by the mentor to extend his or her teaching responsibilities to include work with a new member of the profession. A mentor needs at least three to five years of teaching experience and demonstrated competence as an effective teacher: a person who has a thorough understanding of the school, of the curriculum, of learning theories, of growth and development, of principles of learning, and of evaluation procedures. In addition, equally important is for the mentor to have the respect of fellow faculty and to have the ability to initiate change in the curriculum and school.

The mentor position carries many responsibilities. One of the first is to attend university-sponsored training sessions for mentor teachers. These training sessions assist the mentor in understanding and identifying the purposes of the Teacher Induction Program as well as procedures for accomplishing these purposes. Specific responsibilities throughout the year include accepting the inductee as a colleague and establishing open communication with the inductee and with other members of the induction team. Another responsibility of the mentor is orienting the inductee to the education setting. This orientation includes an understanding of the line and staff organization, acquaintance with faculty and acquaintance with services available through support personnel. The mentor provides assistance in planning for teaching, which includes preparation of the room, a plan for management of student conduct, and a plan for teaching the classes. Because first-year teachers are insecure, the mentor should provide encouragement and reassurance. Inductees need assistance in assessing their accomplishments in the teaching process, in identifying when learning is taking place, and in determining how to enhance the learning process. Further, because evaluation is difficult for first-year teachers, mentors must provide assistance in this area as well as in self-evaluation as a teacher.

Another important task for the mentor is to serve as a teaching model for the inductee. To prevent the frequent isolation and insulation of the novice, time must be provided for mutual observation by mentor and inductee. The observations are profitable because they are followed by planned conferences.

Additional duties of mentor teachers are identified in Figure 2.

Figure 2
Responsibilities of Mentor Teachers

---

1. Assist the inductee in:
   a. understanding the nature of the learners;
   b. understanding the curriculum and resources available for use in the subject/grade level;
   c. understanding the total school program.
2. Serve as a resource for the inductee
   a. by planning for teaching:
      (1)   How much can be covered in a specified time?
      (2)   How much can be expected from the students?
      (3)   What can be expected from the wide variety of learners?
   b. by informing inductees of administrative reports;
   c. by identifying sources of information about teaching, the school, and community.

To assist the mentor teacher in assuming these responsibilities, the university provides a tuition-free three credit graduate course for mentor teachers. The major emphasis of the course is to explore the role of the mentor teacher, to identify the characteristics of an effective teacher, to develop conference techniques with the inductee in self-evaluation procedures, and to become proficient in supervisory methods.

The university provides a second course for mentor teachers, which also carries graduate credit. The emphasis of the second course in on effective teachering and supervision. In the second course, mentors conduct an in-depth study of effective teaching procedures, model these procedures, and analyze teaching through observation.

The university consultant's contribution to the Induction Support Team includes providing professional expertise in the teaching methodology and learning theories for the inductee, providing assistance to the mentor and inductee through monthly on-site conferences, and providing support for the inductere in self-evaluation and personal planning.

All four team members—inductee, administrator, mentor teacher, and university specialist—meet before school starts for a program orientation session organized and sponsored by the university. The purposes of this orientation session are listed in Figure 3.

Figure 3
Orientation Session Objectives

1. To acquaint the team members with the philosophy and goals of the program.
2. To begin planning for action in the classroom, which includes an explanation of the curriculum, development of lesson plans for the start of school, development of a plan for management of student conduct and a plan for student evaluation.
3. To review principles of learning and the anatomy of a lesson.
4. To identify effective relationships in the school setting.
5. To identify the channels of effective communication in a school setting.

The orientation session acquaints all participants with the mentoring program and establishes the communication and planning necessary to assist the first-year teachers in preparing for the start of the school year. In this orientation session, the inductee initiates the Personal Development Plan, which provides an opportunity to identify concerns about teaching in six major categories. After the concerns have been identified, the mentor and university specialist confer with the inductee to establish priority among these concerns and to suggest or recommend methods and information to help in addressing the concerns. This Personal Development Plan becomes a continuous working document during the first year. Through the Plan, the inductee is encouraged to seek assistance from the mentor teacher on a day-to-day basis, and at daily or weekly conferences, and from the university specialist by weekly written reports and monthly on-site visitations. At the monthly on-site visitation, the accomplishments of the first-year teacher are reviewed with the mentor and inductee. As a result of this conference, the inductee can identify areas of growth as a teacher and establish goals for increasing effectiveness.

To assist the induction team, the Domains of the Florida Performance Measurement System have been used by the program developers. The domains are (a) planning, (b) management of student conduct, (c) instructional organization and development, (d) presentation of subject matter, (e) communication, and (f) testing. The teams are encouraged to utilize these domains to establish goals for the inductee and to provide a common definition of effective teaching.

In addition to the monthly on-site visitation by the university specialist, monthly seminars are held to assist the team. The topics of the seminars are management of student conduct, evaluation, parent conferencing, anatomy of a lesson, motivation, and dealing with exceptional learners. All members of the induction team are encouraged to attend these seminars to review the progress of the inductee and to plan for future growth.

FINANCIAL ARRANGEMENTS

School systems that have employed an inexperienced teacher may voluntarily participate in the Teacher Induction Program. The contractual arrangement between the school and the first-year teacher is in accord with the master contract of the school district, with salary commensurate with load. Additional costs to the participating school consist of $600 of in-service monies. These monies are divided equally between in-service activities developed for the benefit of the local school participants and broad-based in-service activities sponsored by the university for the benefit of all participants.

The first-year teacher is admitted to the Graduate School and enrolls for three to six credits of graduate work for each semester, credits that may be applied toward a master's degree.

University costs consist of (a) administration, (b) faculty time for supervision, (c) seminars, (d) $200 per inductee for the broad-based in-service fund, (e) research and program evaluation, (f) graduate credit for mentor training courses, (g) the program orientation seminar, and (h) other incidental costs.

RESEARCH DESIGN

An experimental design was developed by Linda Parker to study the University of Wisconsin-Whitewater Teacher Induction Program during the 1984-85 academic year.[1] The design included twelve inductees as the experimental group and a control group of twelve randomly selected first-year teachers who were not in an induction program. The objectives of the experiment were to describe and evaluate the effectiveness of the mentor/inductee development program and to describe and evaluate the effectiveness of a teacher induction program designed to provide assistance for and support to first-year teachers. To accomplish these objectives, the following procedures were used:

1. *Structured interviews*—A series of three in-depth interviews with every first-year teacher in both groups was conducted to document each teacher's progress through the first year of teaching. These interviews focused on (a) the kinds of problems experienced by the first-year teacher, (b) the kinds and sources of assistance provided to the teacher, (c) perceptions regarding strengths and weaknesses in the assistance provided, (d) perceived effects of the assistance on the beginner's teaching practices and his or her ability to solve problems, and (e) assessments of how the program might have been improved.
2. *Questionnaire*—All persons involved in the delivery of service to the first-year teachers were surveyed to determine their satisfaction with the program, their perceptions regarding the program's strengths and weaknesses, and their suggestions on how the program might be improved.

RESEARCH FINDINGS

Findings from the research were:

1. All 12 members of the experimental group completed the 1984-85

---

[1]More detailed information regarding methodology, data collection, and data analysis procedures may be obtained by contacting the authors.

academic year; only 10 of the 12 control group participants completed the first year of teaching.

2. Nine of the experimental group teachers indicated they planned to be teaching in five years; only 3 of the 12 control group subjects indicated they planned to be teaching in five years.

3. The problems experienced by both groups of beginning teachers were very similar in nature; however, inductees had less difficulty in motivating students, had more success in responding to student misbehaviors, and had more positive relationships with their students.

4. Resolution of problems of first-year teachers can take place in a program that provides assistance to and support for the new teacher.

5. Inductees described their first year of teaching in more positive terms than did the control group.

6. Inductees described themselves as teachers in terms of specific teaching behaviors. Control subjects described themselves more often in terms of attitudes and personal qualities.

Finally, the results of this study suggested that observation and feedback on the beginning teachers' performance by experienced teachers/mentors are helpful and would be welcomed by most first-year teachers.

Administrators involved in the Teacher Induction Program indicated:

1. Fewer problems with the first-year teachers when they were working with the induction program—fewer student referrals, fewer parent calls, fewer student complaints;

2. A close working relationship between first-year teachers and the mentors was a primary reason for fewer problems; and

3. New possibilities for experienced teachers to serve as mentors and to experience the in-services that were offered.

Other findings were:

1. Most of the mentors (11 of 12) enjoyed working with the first-year teachers.

2. All principals in the experimental group schools indicated the program was effective in their schools because of the assistance for the first-year teacher and the professional stimulation for the mentor teacher.

3. Nine of the 12 mentors reported the need for more shared time between mentor and inductee.

4. The orientation period should provide training regarding the goals of the program and the roles of mentor and inductee. Furthermore, time should be provided for the induction team to begin a plan of action for the first-year teacher.

SUMMARY

A collaborative teacher induction program can be an effective means of strengthening the performance of a beginning teachers. The major purposes of the experience are to help beginning teachers develop security and confidence that will improve their teaching, to encourage them to remain in the profession, and to eliminate the isolation they might experience. As a concomitant benefit, a planned interactive in-service program for all participating staff will yield value for inductees, mentors, administrators, and university consultants. This interaction provides university personnel with an opportunity for direct involvement in the transition from pre-service teacher education to in-service teacher development and provides university faculty with an opportunity to study the specific daily needs of first-year teachers. On a broader scale, the experience may be viewed as an effort to improve the teaching profession by retaining the most effective teachers and, ultimately, to improve the quality of education in the nation's schools.

REFERENCES

Bush, R. N. 1983. *The beginning years of teaching: A focus for collaboration in teacher education.* Paper presented at the World Assembly of the International Council on Education for Teaching (30th), Washington, DC.

Dillon-Peterson, E. 1982. Sameness drives me up a wall. In *Beginning teacher induction: Five dilemmas,* ed. G. Hall, 67-77. Austin, TX: University of Texas at Austin, Research and Development Center for Teacher Education.

Dropkin, S., and Taylor, M. 1963. Perceived problems of beginning teachers and related factors. *Journal of Teacher Education* 14: 384-90.

Elias, P.; Fisher, M. L.; and Simon, R. 1980. *Helping beginning teachers through the first year: A review of the literature.* Princeton, NJ: Educational Testing Service.

Elsner, K. 1984. *First year evaluation results from Oklahoma's entry-year assistance committees.* Paper presented at the annual meeting of the Association of Teacher Educators (64th), New Orleans, LA.

Eye, G. G. 1956. *The new teacher comes to school.* New York: Harper.

Grant, C. A., and Zeichner, K. M. 1981. Inservice support for beginning teachers: The state of the scene. *Journal of Research and Development in Education* 14 (2); 99-111.

Griffin, G. A. 1982. Induction—an overview. In *Beginning teacher induction: Five dilemmas*, ed. G. E. Hall, 7-14. Austin, TX: University of Texas at Austin, Research and Development Center for Teacher Education.

_____. 1985. Teacher induction: Research issues. *Teacher Education* 36 (1): 42-46.

Griffin, G. A., and Hukill, H. 1983. Teacher induction issues: Themes and variations. In *First years of teaching: What are the pertinent issues?*, ed. G. A. Griffin and H. Hukill, 107-27. Austin, TX: University of Texas at Austin, Research and Development Center for Teacher Education.

Hall, G. E. 1982. Induction: The missing link. *Journal of Teacher Education* 33 (3): 53-55.

Houston, R.; Piper, M.; Hollis, L.; and Selder, B. 1979. *Problems and perspectives of beginning teachers; A follow-up study.* Houston, TX: University of Houston, Central Campus.

Howsam, R. B; Corrigan, D.; Denemark, G.; and Nash, R. 1976. *Educating a profession.* Washington, DC: American Association of Colleges for Teacher Education.

Lortie, D. C. 1975. *Schoolteacher: A sociological study.* Chicago: University of Chicago Press.

McDonald, F. J. 1980a. *The problems of beginning teachers: A crisis in training.* Princeton, NJ: Educational Testing Service.

McDonald, F. J. 1980b. The teaching internship and teacher induction. In *Assuring qualified educational personnel in the eighties*, ed. C. C. Mackey, Jr., 91-117. Proceedings of the annual convention of the National Association of State Directors of Teacher Education and Certification (52nd) Boston, MA.

Ryan, K. 1970. *Don't smile until Christmas.* Chicago: University of Chicago Press.

_____. 1974. *Survival is not good enough: Overcoming the problems of beginning teachers.* Washington, DC: American Federation of Teachers.

Ryan, K.; Newman, K. K.; Mager, G.; Applegate, J.; Lesley, T.; Flora, R.; and Johnston, J. 1980. *Biting the apple: Accounts of first year teachers.* New York: Longman.

Sandefur, J. T. 1982. What happens to the teacher during induction? In *Beginning teacher induction: Five dilemmas*, ed. G. E. Hall, 41-46. Austin, TX: University of Texas at Austin, Research and Development Center for Teacher Education.

Schlechty, P. C. 1985. A framework for evaluating induction into teaching. *Journal of Teacher Education* 36 (1); 37-41.

Tisher, R. P. 1982. *Teacher induction: An international perspective on research and programs.* Paper presented at the annual meeting of the American Eduational Research Association, New York, NY.

University of Wisconsin System Teacher Education Task Force. 1984. *Benchmarks of excellence: Recommendations of the University of Wisconsin system task force on teacher education.* Madison, WI: University of Wisconsin System.

Veenman, S. 1984. Perceived problems of beginning teachers. *Review of Educational Research* 54 (2): 143-78.

Wisconsin Department of Public Instruction. 1984. *Final report of the state superintendent's task force on teaching and teacher education.* Madison, WI: State of Wisconsin, Department of Public Instruction.

9. THE EFFECTS OF A PLANNED INDUCTION PROGRAM ON FIRST-YEAR TEACHERS: A RESEARCH REPORT

by Alvah M. Kilgore and Julia A. Kozisek

STATEMENT OF THE RESEARCH PROBLEM

The purpose of this chapter is to present the findings of a college/university-based first-year teacher support/induction program on beginning teachers. Given the fact that school-based induction programs for new teachers were few and far between, and that NCATE indicated that colleges have an obligation to provide support to their graduates, a program was developed to answer the following questions:

1. What is the perceived knowledge base held by first-year teachers, before and after their first year of teaching?
2. What are administrator perceptions of the skills of first-year teachers?
3. What are the first-year teachers' expectations and realities concerning teaching before and after their first year of teaching?
4. What kind of in-school support was provided to teachers during their first year of teaching (e.g., principal, peers, mentors)?
5. What were the effects of a college-level support program on the first-year teacher?

DESCRIPTION OF THE INTERVENTION PROGRAM

Teachers College, University of Nebraska, Concordia Teachers College, and Doane College, all in the state of Nebraska and part of a statewide consortium, developed and implemented a first-year teacher support program from the higher education perspective. The program included a selection of students from each college who participated in a summer graduate program, a first-year on-site visitation program, and regional seminars. Participants received direct help in finding a teaching position, acceptance into a master's program with completion of at least nine hours of credit by the end of their first teaching year, help in preparing for their first year of teaching, assignment of a mentor teacher, on-site visits by college personnel, and employers were provided with a "warrant" indicating that the teacher would perform well in the classroom.

Teachers participated in two, three-credit-hour workshop seminars during the summer after graduation and preceding their first year of teaching. The first workshop was used to assess a variety of skill levels of the participants (e.g., organizational ability, planning, problem analysis, judgment, decisiveness, sensitivity, and written communication), and to provide experiences and further skill development in observation, testing and test construction, socialization of first-year teachers, as well as in planning and learning to anticipate situations that might occur during their first year of teaching. Participants were also expected to make site visits, gather information, textbooks, schedules, assignments, curricula, etc., and to bring back specific information about the community and school in which they were going to work.

The second workshop consisted of the application of planning and the production of materials that would enhance the participants' first year of teaching. Included were such items as a yearly calendar, bulletin boards, lesson plans for the first two weeks of school, a curriculum outline for the year, teacher-made tests and quizzes, a discipline plan, tansparencies and other media to enhance instruction, and plans for developing and reporting grades. The objective was to try to have as many questions about the school year answered as possible to lessen the "shock" of reality that would accompany their first year of teaching.

RESEARCH DESIGN

The research design for the first group that entered the program was a pre-post, nonrandom field-based experimental-control group format, using pretest data as a covariate to balance group differences. Control group participants consisted of teachers meeting all program entry requirements and invited to participate, but who, for one reason or another, decided not to be in the program. Twenty-two teachers made up the experimental group and completed the first year of the program. The data were completed for twenty-two experimental group and eighteen control group teachers.

Both quantitative and qualitative data were collected during the course of the study. Presage data included participant completion of the *Adjective Checklist*, primarily to act as a covariate, When pre- and post-test scores were applied, there were no differences between groups, and the summer and year of teaching made no statistically significant difference between groups, nor did their views of themselves change, at least as indicated by using this instrument.

94

Additional presage data included completion of an instrument that had the teachers indicate what they perceived their level of knowledge and competency on selected teaching behaviors to be. The teaching behaviors represented the major areas reported in the research on teaching studies in which first-year teachers experience problems. The principal of each participant was also asked to rate the competency of each teacher using the same instrument that the teacher used, and the teachers were asked to rerate themselves at the end of their first year of teaching. Teachers were also asked to respond to a questionnaire that asked for their expectations of selected working conditions prior to teaching, and the realities of their situation (as opposed to their expectations) at the end of their first year (Marso and Pigge 1986).

Qualitative data were collected in three ways. First, participants were asked to keep a weekly log during their first year of teaching. The log required entries that followed a format provided by the researchers and covered a variety of events that occurred to the participants. For purposes of this study, log entries from the first and last six weeks of the first year of teaching were compared. The second method used to collect qualitative data were observations made while on-site by the researchers during visits to teachers throughout their first year of teaching. Notes were kept and analyzed upon return to campus. Third, teachers participated in regional seminars held during the second semester of their first year of teaching. Notes taken from the seminars comprised this part of the qualitative data collection.

RESULTS: QUANTITATIVE ANALYSES

1. Both groups of teachers began and ended the first year reporting a high level of teaching skill. Although the experimental group's self-reported skills did increase across time, there was not a statistically significant difference between the two groups. The experimental group's perceived level of teaching skill appeared to increase after the summer experience, and then decreased after completion of the first year. Even with this perceived skill decrease, the reported level of skill was still higher than at the beginning of the year (Table 1). Based on this decrease reported by the experimental group of teachers, one might conclude either that the public school experience is having a negative impact on these teachers or that the summer program produced a false sense of efficacy that was lowered on contact with the school experience. The control group remained relatively stable across the year.

2. Both groups of teachers entered the first year with expectations

95

that were not met. The experimental group's expectations actually increased after the summer experience. They left the summer experience expecting several of the working conditions to be more positive than when they began the summer. Once in the school, the teachers discovered that what they expected to happen was not necessarily true. The teachers experienced "reality shock." A conflict appears to exist between what the first-year teacher expected and the reality of the situation (Tables 2 and 3).

3. When both groups of teachers were assessed by their principals' perceptions of skill level (a postassessment only), there were no differences noted between groups. Generally, the principals found all the teachers to be highly competent.

4. Further analyses compared the self-rating of teachers with the ratings given them by their principals (Table 4). First-year teachers and principals did not have the same perceptions of the elements that are necessary for teaching effectiveness. Principals were not looking at the same skills as the teachers when defining success. Principals need to be aware of teachers' expectations and definitions concerning teaching effectiveness as well as their own.

5. Similar support services appeared to be offered to both groups of first-year teachers, although the support was not at a very high level. Seventy-seven percent of experimental group teachers did have a mentor teacher appointed, as opposed to 11 percent of the control group (although not all mentor teachers fulfilled a true mentoring role). Over 90 percent of experimental group teachers received information from their principals before and during their first year, as opposed to about 60 percent of the control group. Although some other differences were noted between how first-year teachers were supported, what was noticeable was the lack of any consistent support services for either group on important issues. For example, teachers in neither group received much feedback on their performance early in the year from principals and supervisors; teachers were not given lighter loads, or released time to plan, or were not assigned fewer nonteaching responsibilities; time was not provided to observe and work with veteran teachers or to help with administrative paperwork; and activities were not specifically directed toward their needs, such as in-service programs and the development of personal development plans. All in all, outside of a little more information at the beginning of the year and a mentor teacher assigned, little difference was noted in the support treatment given to first-year teachers (Table 5). The first-year teacher was treated the same as the veteran teacher of 20 years.

Table 1
The Perceived Knowledge Base Held by First-Year Teachers:
Posttest Comparisons:
Control and Experimental Groups

| | Control | | Experimental | | |
| | Posttest N = 18 | | Posttest N = 22 | | |
Knowledge Statement	X	SD	X	SD	t
1. Classroom discipline	4.89	0.90	5.32	0.65	−1.87
2. Classroom management	5.28	0.67	5.23	0.75	+0.24
3. Motivating students	5.33	0.84	5.05	0.59	+1.33
4. Dealing with individual differences	4.67	1.03	4.95	0.95	−0.96
5. Evaluation of students	5.06	0.94	5.05	0.95	+0.03
6. Relationships with parents	5.56	0.92	5.41	0.80	+0.58
7. Organization of the classroom	5.44	0.92	5.50	1.14	−0.19
8. Organization of own time	5.11	1.13	5.14	1.08	−0.09
9. Teaching techniques/methods	5.28	0.57	5.50	0.67	−1.22
10. Subject matter specific to area	5.28	0.46	5.36	0.73	−0.42
11. Planning and organizing	5.39	1.20	5.60	1.01	−0.64
12. Paperwork, records, reports	5.61	1.04	4.95	1.07	+2.06[a]
13. First day of school	4.61	1.20	5.05	0.84	−1.47
14. Use of curriculum guides texts, materials, and resources	5.00	0.77	5.32	0.95	−1.14
15. Communications with administrators, colleagues, students, parents	5.35	0.93	5.59	1.10	−0.77
16. Relationships with administrators, colleagues, students	5.72	0.96	5.66	1.11	+0.19
Overall perception of being a teacher	5.39	0.61	5.36	0.56	+0.18

[a]$p > 0.05$.
Preface each statement with: "The degree to which I feel competent in:"
Scale used: 1 = no confidence:: 7 = very high level of confidence.

Table 2
Expectations and Realities: Pre- and Posttest Comparisons of First-Year Teachers on Selected Criteria: Experimental Group

Expectation/Reality Statement	Expectation Pretest N = 22		Reality Posttest N = 22		
	X	SD	X	SD	t
WORKING CONDITIONS					
Instructional help/guidance/advice from:					
1. Other teachers	5.82	0.85	5.59	0.80	+0.85
2. Administrators/supervisors/chairs	5.82	0.66	4.91	1.31	+3.03[a]
3. In-service training	5.32	1.09	3.86	1.53	+4.29[b]
4. College coursework/experiences	6.00	0.76	6.05	0.59	−0.20
Rapport with and respect of:					
5. Students	6.36	0.66	6.23	0.87	+0.50
6. Parents of students	6.00	0.76	5.73	0.98	+0.96
7. Other teachers	6.05	0.72	5.95	1.00	+0.36
8. Administrators/supervisors/chairs	6.09	0.53	5.55	1.14	+2.16[a]
9. Community members	5.95	0.79	5.27	1.12	+2.52[a]
10. Budgetary support for my teaching area	4.95	1.21	4.36	1.53	+1.51
Support (and encouragement) of my teaching area from:					
11. Parents	5.50	0.96	5.27	1.39	+0.67
12. Other teachers	5.82	0.80	5.55	0.96	+1.12
13. Administrators	5.82	0.73	5.41	1.18	+1.46
14. Community members	5.27	0.83	5.05	1.13	+0.79
15. Physical facilities for my teaching area	5.18	1.10	4.95	1.56	+0.68
16. Equipment and materials for my teaching area	5.14	1.13	4.50	1.71	+1.56
17. Parent-Teacher conferences	5.55	0.80	5.52	1.17	+0.10
18. Scheduling of classes (or class time) to complete desired Objectives	5.32	0.89	5.33	1.24	−0.03

Table 2 (*Continued*)
Expectations and Realities: Pre- and Posttest Comparisons
of First-Year Teachers on Selected Criteria:
Experimental Group

Expectation/Reality Statement	Expectation Pretest N = 22		Reality Posttest N = 22		
	X	SD	X	SD	t
19. An environment that is conducive to professional growth and development	5.64	0.85	5.05	1.16	+1.97
20. Feelings of accomplishment	5.82	0.85	5.24	1.26	+1.93
21. Work load (time, energy needed, number of students, classes, etc.)	5.82	0.91	4.14	1.75	+4.94[b]
22. Behavior of students	5.36	1.00	5.09	1.15	+0.87
23. My teaching being observed by administrators	5.73	0.77	5.10	1.55	+1.97
24. Level of satisfaction	6.14	0.71	5.59	1.13	+1.96
25. Job orientation	5.77	0.75	5.05	1.07	+2.40[a]

[a]$P > 0.05$; [b]$P > 0.01$.

Scale used: 1 = low expectation or reality:: 7 = very high expectation or reality.

Table 3
Expectations and Realities: Pre- and Posttest Comparisons
of First-Year Teachers on Selected Criteria:
Control Group

Expectation/Reality Statement	Expectation Pretest N = 18		Reality Posttest N = 18		
	X	SD	X	SD	t
WORKING CONDITIONS Instructional help/guidance/advice from:					
1. Other teachers	5.67	0.77	5.56	1.33	+0.32
2. Administrators/supervisors/chairs	5.67	1.28	4.94	1.47	+1.87[a]
3. In-service training	5.61	0.85	4.06	1.47	+4.43[b]
4. College coursework/experiences	5.44	1.04	5.39	1.33	+0.14
Rapport with and respect of:					
5. Students	6.39	0.70	6.28	0.83	+0.38
6. Parents of students	6.11	0.96	5.78	0.94	+0.41
7. Other teachers	6.11	0.68	6.06	0.94	+0.17
8. Administrators/supervisors/chairs	6.11	0.96	5.28	1.45	+2.18[a]
9. Community members	5.78	1.00	5.00	1.17	+2.29[a]
10. Budgetary support for my teaching area	4.78	1.31	4.76	1.23	+0.05
Support (and encouragement) of my teaching area from:					
11. Parents	5.22	0.94	5.41	1.06	−0.58
12. Other teachers	5.72	0.75	5.71	1.05	+0.03
13. Administrators	5.89	0.83	5.12	1.54	+1.97
14. Community members	5.22	0.88	4.88	1.11	+1.10
15. Physical facilities for my teaching area	5.50	0.86	5.06	1.39	+1.20
16. Equipment and materials for my teaching area	5.61	0.92	5.06	1.55	+1.49
17. Parent-Teacher conferences	5.67	1.08	5.44	1.10	+0.66
18. Scheduling of classes (or class time) to complete desired objectives	5.39	1.09	4.56	1.42	+2.07[a]
19. An environment that is conducive to professional growth and development	5.70	0.82	5.22	1.40	+1.37

Table 3 (*Continued*)
Expectations and Realities: Pre- and Posttest Comparisons
of First-Year Teachers on Selected Criteria:
Control Group

| | Expectation | | Reality | | |
| | Pretest N = 18 | | Posttest N = 18 | | |
Expectation/Reality Statement	X	SD	X	SD	t
20. Feelings of accomplishment	6.06	0.64	5.22	1.31	$+2.62^{a}$
21. Work load (time, energy needed, number of students, classes, etc.)	4.89	1.41	4.28	1.90	$+1.17$
22. Behavior of students	5.50	1.04	5.17	1.29	$+0.92$
23. My teaching being observed by administrators	5.67	0.91	4.78	1.90	$+1.89$
24. Level of satisfaction	6.17	0.62	5.39	1.29	$+2.44^{a}$
25. Job orientation	5.44	0.86	4.83	1.50	$+1.56$

[a]$P>0.05$; [b]$P>0.01$.
Scale used: 1 = low expectation or reality:: 7 = very high expectation or reality.

Table 4
Administrator Perceptions of First-Year Teachers'
Performances on Knowledge Base Criteria:
Posttest Only Comparisons

Knowledge Statement	Control		Experimental		
	Pretest N = 15		Posttest N = 23		
	X	SD	X	SD	t
1. Classroom discipline	5.20	0.67	5.21	0.78	+0.04
2. Classroom management	5.47	0.64	0.38	0.77	−0.41
3. Motivating students	5.53	0.92	5.71	0.86	+0.29
4. Dealing with individual differences	5.13	0.35	5.46	0.83	+1.57
5. Evaluation of students	5.47	0.92	5.38	0.71	+0.03
6. Relationships with parents	5.71	0.61	5.38	0.82	+1.43
7. Organization of the classrrom	5.73	0.59	5.75	0.79	+0.09
8. Organization of own time	5.60	0.74	5.71	0.81	+0.44
9. Teaching techniques/methods	5.67	0.90	5.71	0.95	+0.14
10. Subject matter specific to area	5.47	1.13	6.00	0.78	+1.83
11. Planning and organizing	5.73	0.96	5.83	0.82	+0.35
12. Paperwork, records, reports	5.67	0.62	5.63	0.65	−0.25
13. First day of school	5.40	0.63	5.71	0.55	+1.72
14. Use of curriculum guides, texts, materials, and resources	5.60	0.74	5.67	0.56	+0.35
15. Communications with administrators, colleagues, students, parents	6.00	0.65	5.69	0.72	−1.49
16. Relationships with administrators, colleagues, students	6.13	0.64	5.79	0.88	−1.36
Overall perception of being a teacher	5.57	0.94	5.58	0.76	+0.04

[a]P>0.05;
Preface each statement with: "The degree to which the teacher is competent in." Scale used:
1 = no skill: 7 = very high level of skill.

Table 5
Support Received by First-Year Teachers During
Their First Year of Teaching

Type of Support	Experimental N = 22		Control N = 18	
	Number	Percent	Number	Percent
1. Assigned to a mentor teacher	17	77	2	11
2. Met with principal prior to school to receive information about district, school policies and philosophy, curriculum, calendar, schedules, etc.	20	91	13	59
3. Received a teaching assignment for which you were qualified and prepared	22	100	15	83
4. Took part in a separate in-service/ orientation just for new teachers at the beginning of the year	14	64	12	66
5. Received a preschool orientation to school, community, etc.	8	36	8	44
6. Introduced to other faculty before school started	20	91	12	66
7. Invited to social gatherings	18	82	14	77
8. Informal visits by the principal early in the year	11	50	9	50
9. Met with local teachers association	12	55	9	50
10. Received personalized notes/feed-back from the principal early in the year	8	36	9	50
11. Given released time to observe other teachers, plan for classes, etc.	8	36	7	39
12. Given a reduced workload	2	9	1	6
13. Given a reduced class size	3	14	0	0
14. Assigned fewer nonteaching responsibilities	6	27	3	17
15. Provided with in-class assistance	5	23	2	11

Table 5 (continued)
Support Received by First-Year Teachers During
Their First Year of Teaching

Type of Support	Experimental N = 22		Control N = 18	
	Number	Percent	Number	Percent
16. Provided with time to talk to other beginning teachers	6	27	3	17
17. In-service specifically directed toward the new teacher	1	5	4	22
18. Demonstration lessons from master teachers	3	14	3	17
19. Orientation to the procedures for supervision and evaluation	10	45	9	50
20. Observations by the principal	19	86	14	77
21. Feedback by the principal	18	82	15	83
22. Development of a personal development plan to specifically meet your needs as a teacher	4	18	6	33
23. Videotaping of you teaching, with time to review and critique	1	5	0	0
24. Help with administrative paperwork	3	14	2	11
25. Other:				
student assistants			1	6
departmental aide			1	6

RESULTS: QUALITATIVE DATA

Teacher Journals

First-year teachers in the experimental group were asked to keep a weekly log. They were provided with an outline for the log with the following categories: (1) life in the classroom; (2) life in the school; (3) life in extracurricular activities; (4) feelings for the week; and (5) future plans based on the week. Log entries from the first and last six weeks of the school year were analyzed for this study. General concepts were identified from a content-analysis framework.

There were several topics that emerged from the content analysis of both the beginning and ending entries. They were—

1. The students;
2. Planning/use of time;
3. The mentor teacher;
4. The principal;
5. Classroom management;
6. The parents;
7. Extracurricular duties/activities;
8. Relationships with others;
9. Curriculum;
10. Professional roles; and
11. General and personal feelings.

Additionally, early entries included first day (and week) feelings, the new teacher orientation sessions and organizing the classroom. Two categories appeared in the end-of-year entries that were not mentioned in the early entries. The first area concerned instruction. Many of the first-year teachers wrote about wanting to find new ways to meet objectives and keep students motivated and interested. They felt that they might be getting into a rut and that things were starting to drag. Several noted that they were trying to work on games, activities, and other ideas to deal with their concerns. The final category mentioned in the end-of-year entries included future plans for the teachers. Concerns were raised about "next year." There was talk of one school closing and employment status was unclear. Several teachers were getting married and did not know where they would have to relocate. Searching for a new teaching job was a topic in several journals.

On-Site Visits

As part of the program, each first-year teacher was visited (at least twice) by a college professor or representative. The visits included time spent observing the teacher and talking with the principal, the mentor teacher, and the first-year teacher. Observation data provided non-threatening feedback to the teachers as well as some positive strokes and the sight of a "friendly" face. The familiar face of the college professor was a welcome sight, with hugs and smiles from the teacher common elements of the visits. Suggestions and help offered were appreciated by the teachers as they indicated that they had not received much support or feedback from their mentors and principals. Informal time was also spent with the teachers, providing them with a listening ear and a sounding board. Many problems and questions that the teacher was afraid to ask the principal were shared and solved during the informal conference. Some principals made an attempt to observe the teacher prior to the visit so that they could share their views with the college representative, but this was the exception rather than the rule.

Discussions with the mentor teachers revealed that many had no idea of what it was they were supposed to do to help the first-year teacher. (Principals had been sent letters and specific information concerning the role and responsibilities of the mentor teacher and asked to share this information with mentors. Many of the mentors had not received the information.) Most of the time spent with the mentor teachers centered around suggestions and activities that they could do with and for the beginners. As the on-site visits stretched out over the first semester, valuable time had been lost in building a working relationship between the mentor and the teacher. Some mentors, on their own initiative, had taken an active role with the teachers. Then, the visit was one of talking about what they had done so far and offering other ideas as necessary. At times, it was also evident that there was little open communication between the principal, the mentor, and the first-year teacher. As a result, the on-site visits by college personnel often provided an important link between the principal, the mentor teacher and the first-year teacher.

Seminar Sessions

During the second semester of their first year, the teachers were asked to participate in field-based seminars. The purpose of the seminars was to provide a structure through which the teachers could discuss and REFLECT on some of their first-year experiences. Many of the teachers had not been able to discuss experiences and concerns with anyone else, and they appeared eager to share with their peers what was happening to them. Sessions were held from 2:00 p.m. to nine or ten in the evening. Sites were at or near a restaurant so that the discussions could continue over dinner. Questions were posed by the college representative that tried to elicit specific feedback and isolate any problems as seen by the teachers. Notes were taken at each session and assessed after the session. Based on a summary of the four seminars held with these teachers, the research team has synthesized the following areas of concern for the first-year teachers:

1. Teachers were very frustrated, and felt unprepared to deal with the wide range of student abilities, habits, and behaviors that were encountered in every classroom (from familial situations of having children from homes with dirt floors to high-income homes in the same classroom; to having behaviorally impaired children in the mainstream, etc.). Many questioned their ability to reach all of the students.

2. There was a general disappointment with the manner, attitudes, and professionalism of their more experienced peers. The general feeling was that most teachers seemed to be negative (cynical) about their jobs, the children in the school, the lack of support and supplies, the loads carried, relationships, and so on. Lounge and lunchroom talk led some of the first-year teachers to isolate themselves from the rest of the faculty, eating in their classrooms and not attending social functions.

3. There was concern about the "socialization" that was taking place in the school, how the various messages were being received and how the hidden norms of the schools were shared. Many teacher were put into uncomfortable positions because no one informed them of possible consequences of their decisions before these decisions were made. For instance, one teacher left the building during a free period to get a hamburger at a fast food establishment. Upon returning with his sack, he was met by the secretary who admonished him quite severely—he didn't leave the building any more. Another teacher, during the holiday season, asked permission to put up some decorations in her classroom. Permission was granted, and after she had spent the better part of a weekend getting the room in a holiday/learning mode, a colleague who walked in on Monday loudly berated and condemned her, and went to other teachers with her complaints. As a result, the principal (from whom permission was originally granted) asked her to take down most of the decorations. Some of the ideas and reflections that dealt with the socialization process appear to be connected with the first-year teachers'

perceptions of their more experienced peers in general; however, the two issues appear to be different enough to state as separate concerns.

4. Finally, the role of the mentor and principal was discussed by the teachers. Not having taught before, these teachers had no comparison base to turn to when describing their relationships with principals and teachers. What appeared to emerge from listening to their discussions of the roles the principals and mentors played led the researchers to believe that: principal support was not obvious, nor was any type of evaluative help (in general). Principals just did not get around to these teachers very often. They were left to their own devices (although the teachers were not necessarily negative about their principals, they were seen as someone more distant and with little direct influences on them). Support from the mentor teachers varied, from high involvement and support in one case, to several having no mentor assigned, or a mentor assigned but with no action or support given. In several cases, the new teachers sought out someone closer to their own age and experience level and attempted to develop a relationship with him or her.

5. The teachers expressed gratitude in being able to gather together and talk with other first-year teachers. As one shared: "It's nice to know that there are people going through some of the same troubles I am." It was reassuring to them that their problems were not unique to just them. One teacher left feeling her situation was not nearly as bad as she originally thought after she heard others describe theirs. It was a valuable experience for them to share ideas and talk with other teachers about the ways that they were handling their situations.

CONCLUSIONS AND RECOMMENDATIONS

The data collected and analyzed from quantitative measures along with the findings from the three types of qualitative data appear to build a rather convincing picture of the tenuous life of a first-year teacher, even when the teacher is provided with a college-based support program. If it were not for the extremely high level of self-confidence and high expectations that a beginning teacher has, one might predict that the number of teachers that leave the profession would be higher than it is at present. Teachers who participated in this study, whether in the support program or not, began the summer and ended the year reporting a high level of teaching skill. These teachers believed in themselves, although they did not always receive the feedback to confirm their beliefs. This efficacy, real or imagined, appears to be a necessary ingredient in the makeup of a successful novice teacher.

A second general conclusion appears to indicate that the role that college personnel might play in providing support to first-year teachers is probably peripheral rather than direct. The influence of the school environment, peers, and especially the students on an everyday basis is so strong that external intervention techniques make little difference in the behaviors of the teachers. Teachers might be comforted to know that someone comes to visit with them on occasion, and lends a sympathetic ear, but the process is not strong enough to make a difference. The research team does believe, based on certain events, that there is a role for college personnel in this process. The one activity that may have led to some changes in both behavior and thinking of the students was the seminar situation, the time for teachers to pause and reflect upon their experiences. This kind of opportunity does not seem to take place in the very busy world of any teacher, let alone a first-year novice. The second activity that seemed beneficial to a limited extent was the opportunity to visit with principals and mentor teachers about the induction process. For the most part, school personnel are not aware of the literature or effects they have on first-year teachers. Simply stated, principals and teachers treat novice teachers like they were treated, and have had no reason to think that things should be any different. Sharing the research and suggesting practices to help first-year teachers did benefit some of the teachers in the program. However, this seems to be a rather expensive and time-consuming way to get the message to school personnel.

More specifically, some additional conclusions derived from the study include:

1. Job-embedded considerations for first-year teachers such as providing extra planning time, lighter loads; more observation and feedback; released time to visit other classrooms, work with the mentor teacher or talk with other first-year teachers; and exemptions from duties, are not being provided for first-year teachers, nor can a college-based support program provide this type of service.

First-year teachers were not treated differently than the veteran teacher. Beginning teachers should be expected to possess a wide variety of skills but should not be expected to function as master teachers. School officials need to realize that teachers enter with a set of skills that need to be extended, refined, and developed. Job-embedded support is one way to help with the developmental process of becoming a teacher. The impact and role of the schools must be redefined to meet the needs of the first-year teacher.

2. This study confirmed prior research in that the influence of the school environment appears to be a powerful socializing force on first-year teachers. Several factors had an impact upon these teachers: (1) the isolation felt as they were left alone to teach in their own rooms; (2) the lack of support and relationships formed between colleagues; (3) the hidden and unwritten rules of the school; (4) the inability to observe other successful teachers; (5) the lack of differentiation of in-service programs for first-year teachers; and (6) the powerful role that the principal plays. These factors were a part of the shaping process of the first year as the teacher entered an ongoing professional and social community.

3. The principal is a major force in helping to make the transition from student to teacher a successful one. Supervision is needed so that the teachers do not repeat errors. Yet the principals in this study varied in their degree of supervision. A few were actively involved throughout the year, but most were perceived as "invisible" by the first-year teachers. Most of the teachers were left on their own, except for the information they chose to seek. The teachers in the study were disappointed with the lack of administrative assistance and support.

Beginning teachers want and need more direct supervisory assistance, including specific instructional support and suggestions. Without supervision, first-year teachers can become easily overwhelmed and center on survival tactics rather than on effective teaching strategies. Supervision must be increased, with principals taking a more active role. Options for consideration include a staged entry process to meet district expectations and competencies, a career-ladder approach, involvement of college personnel in the supervision process, and the use of videotape to provide feedback. Principals must not see first-year teachers as finished products, but rather as teachers that need continuing supervision and instruction as they develop into master teachers.

4. The role of the mentor teacher as envisioned to be functional, was not fulfilled by mentors in this study. The mentor, in most cases, provided the initial link and information for the novice teacher. But as the school year progressed, the support did not always meet the expectations of the first-year teacher. Mentors were not provided with support by their principal such as extra pay, recognition or training for assuming the duties of a mentor. Some of the first-year teachers questioned the need for having a mentor. Several thought it would be better to seek out their own mentor, someone closer to their own age and interests. This, in fact, happened with several of the first-year teachers during the year.

5. Classroom management did not seem to be a major problem for the teachers in this study, as the literature indicates. The summer program helped the teachers design their discipline/management programs for the first year. This component of the program seems to have been very useful as the teachers shared their use of their management systems. The preparation over the summer appeared to help relieve some of the tension that might have been felt without such a program.

6. Time and structure needs to be provided to the first-year teacher for reflection. Teachers need time to think about events that happen in the classroom; about the differences in their students, and why certain things seem to happen. Beginning teachers need someone to share their thoughts with, who can empathize and share possible solutions to problems. They need to feel that they are part of a larger, caring, and committed faculty with a mission to carry out. The teachers in this study found themselves too often isolated (by design or by choice) from their peers. The journals provided the teachers with an outlet to share their feelings, but they were not able to get the feedback they wanted. The on-site visits provided many of the teachers with their first opportunity to discuss problems and concerns with someone. The regional seminars were effective in allowing the teachers to meet and share common concerns, problems, and ideas. More opportunities need to be planned to allow teachers to reflect about teaching. All teachers could benefit from the chance to talk and reflect with their colleagues.

7. The needs of the first-year teachers appeared to change from the beginning to the end of the year. By the middle of the year, they were secure in their situations and were ready to move on to deal with instructional matters. The teachers were eager for new ideas, methods, and processes to be more effective in their classrooms. Yet, the first-year teachers in the study were asked to take part in the same in-service programs as the rest of the teachers. Principals and mentors must be prepared to deal with the change and growth and to anticipate and prepare for the emerging needs of the first-year teacher. Multiple in-service learning experiences should be provided for teachers to address the varying concerns and problems experienced. This could be done through the use of a personal development plan, an area consortium of schools, and better utilizations of staff within a school district. Beginning teachers need to be provided with the opportunity for continuing instruction based upon their needs, to allow them to grow and develop to their fullest potential.

8. There seemed to be a difference between what the quantitative data reported and what the teachers were sharing qualitatively. Although

major differences were not reported between the groups, the teachers continually remarked how important and beneficial the support program was for them. While it is difficult to quantify the statements, one might conclude that there was some impact as a result of the first-year teacher's involvement in the planned induction and support program. It may be that future research needs to use more of a case-study approach to study certain parts of the induction process.

9. The role of college personnel seems to center on providing external support, offering feedback, and intervening, in some cases, to ease the transition for first-year teachers. Perhaps the role of college personnel should be restructured. One idea would be to put more emphasis on working with principals and faculty to share the knowledge base concerning induction practices. Time could be spent in training principals and mentor teachers to work more effectively with first-year teachers. Another role could be that of providing assistance with seminars for first-year teachers. This would provide the teachers with the opportunity to reflect and make changes in their behavior.

If induction programs are to succeed, the profession as well as the public must be educated concerning the needs of the beginning teacher and the role experienced personnel play in assisting the induction process. A college-based induction and support program is not enough. There is a need for commitment by all personnel involved. Partnerships must be formed between the public schools and colleges. Preparing teachers is a developmental process that requires collaboration and cooperation between the colleges and the public schools. Together, schools and colleges can develop an induction program based on the research that will make a difference in the development of first-year teachers.

Induction programs are not currently meeting the needs of first-year teachers, regardless of where they originate. Time, energy, and thought have not been provided by and for school personnel to carefully consider the implications and benefits that could be derived from school-based induction programs. Some might think this just something else to do in an already hopelessly busy schedule, but the consequences of losing potentially good teachers might be worse.

SELECT BIBLIOGRAPHY

Applegate, J. H.; Flora, V. R.; and Lasley, T. J. 1980. New teachers seek support. *Educational Leadership* 38 (1): 74-76.

Arends, D. G. 1983. Beginning teachers as learners. *Journal of Educational Research* 76 (4): 235-42.

Armstrong, D. G. 1984. New teachers: Why do they leave and how can principals retain them? *NASSP Bulletin* 68 (469): 110-15.

Corcoran, E. 1981. Transition shock: The beginning teacher's paradox. *Journal of Teacher Education* 32 (3): 19-23.

Gorton, R. A. 1973. Comments on research: The beginning teacher. *NASSP Bulletin* 57 (369): 100-108.

Grant, C. A., and Zeichner, K. M. 1981. Inservice support for first-year teachers: The state of the scene. *Journal of Research and Development in Education* 14 (2): 99-111.

Hall, G. E. 1982. Induction: The missing link. *Journal of Teacher Education* 14 (3): 53-55.

Huling-Austin, L. 1985. Teacher induction programs: What is and isn't reasonable to expect. *Research and Development Center for Teacher Education Review* 3 (4-8).

———. 1986. What can and cannot reasonably be expected from teacher induction programs. *Journal of Teacher Education* 37 (2-5).

Kurtz, W. H. 1983. Identifying their need: How the principal can help beginning teachers. *NASSP Bulletin* 67 (459): 42-45.

Marso, R. N., and Pigge, F. L. 1986. *Beginning teachers: Expectations vs. realities.* Paper presented at the 41st annual meeting of the Association for Supervision and Curriculum Development, San Francisco.

Meyers, P. E. 1981. A crucial challenge: The principal and the beginning teacher. *NASSP Bulletin* 65 (444): 70-75.

Ryan, K., et al. 1980. Biting the apple: Accounts of first-year teachers. New York: Longman.

APPENDIX. TEACHER INDUCTION: AN ANNOTATED BIBLIOGRAPHY

by John M. Johnston

Ashburn, Elizabeth A. 1987. Current developments in teacher induction programs. *Action in Teacher Education* 8 (Winter): 41-44. Provides an overview of the induction scene from the need for induction programs, to sources for existing induction programs, to the need for comparative analysis of different types of programs. Written by the Director of the ERIC Clearinghouse of Teacher Education, this article provides a quick overview and useful starting point for further inquiry about teacher induction.

Barnes, Susan. 1987. Assessment issues in initial year of teaching programs. In *The first year of teaching: Background papers and a proposal*, ed. Gary A. Griffin and Suzanne Millies, 115-27. Chicago: University of Illinois-Chicago. Addresses the thorny problem of combining support for and evaluation of beginning teachers. Barnes's purpose is to address selected issues related to the assessment of beginning teachers as a component of an induction program. Her perspective is one of an assessment system operating within the induction program within the political, educational, and social systems in a school system, not in isolation. From this perspective, Barnes discusses policy, technical, and implementation issues encountered in developing an assessment system. The paper includes a brief discussion of the relationship of the assessment system to preservice and in-service training.

Brooks, Douglas, M., ed. 1987. *Teacher induction: A new beginning*. Reston, VA: Association of Teacher Educators. Reports the results of two years of inquiry by members of the Association of Teacher Educators National Commission on the Induction Process. This monograph provides the most up-to-date report available of induction programs and activities currently in progress in local school systems across the country; state induction programs that have been implemented or that are now being piloted; the status of institutions of higher education involvement in beginning teacher induction; and positions on teacher induction of a variety of professional education organizations. It is a timely, highly readable resource that provides an invaluable starting point for surveying the state of current teacher induction practice in the United States.

Burke, Peter, and Notar, Ellen Elms. 1986. The school and the university: Bridging the gap in teacher induction. *Action in Teacher Education* 7 (Winter):

Portions of this Bibliography are adapted from *Reforming Teacher Education: Issues and New Directions*, Joseph A. Braun, Editor, Garland Publishing, New York, 1989.

11-16. Outlines the role of the university in an induction program, along with factions in the university and the school culture that both support and thwart program development. Burke and Notar explore issues in the development of a collaborative teacher induction program, and consider rewards for assisting beginning teachers.

Carter, Kathy, and Koehler, Virginia Richardson. 1987. The process and content of initial year of teaching programs. In *The first year of teaching: Background papers and a proposal,* ed. Gary A. Griffin and Suzanne Millies, 91-104. Chicago: University of Illinois-Chicago. Proposes content and processes for initial year of teaching programs. Carter and Richardson develop the general goals of a beginning teacher program by describing the ways in which beginning teachers differ from both preservice and experienced teachers in terms of knowledge, skill, attitudes, cognitive processes, and their needs in these areas. They lay out a foundation for such a program based on a conception of teaching, of knowledge needs of beginning teachers, and of the learning-to-teach process. Suggests that development and use of a case literature holds particular promise for meeting specific objectives proposed for initial year of teaching programs.

Eddy, Elizabeth M. 1969. *Becoming a teacher: The passage to professional status.* New York: Teachers College Press. Examines the professional development of twenty-two first-year teachers in inner city elementary and junior high schools. Using weekly tape-recorded sessions as a data base, Eddy was able to study classroom events, the experiences of these new teachers, their satisfactions, problems, and changing perceptions. The purpose of this classic and still informative study is "to provide a greater understanding of the social relationships within the school which deeply affect new teachers and their teaching performance and which must be taken into account if teacher education and recruitment is to become more meaningful for those who teach in slum areas" (p. 7).

Eddy uses the anthropological concept of social transition to explore how beginning teachers learn the responsibilities and activities appropriate to their new role. She also uses the concept of rites of passage to examine the experience of beginning teachers as they separate from their secure home and college existence, their transition from student to teacher, and their eventual incorporation as a teacher in a particular school setting. She carefully considers the roles played by administrators, other teachers, students and their parents in shaping the new teachers' professional self-expectations.

Becoming a Teacher is one of the few publications to date that not only chronicles the experiences of the beginning teacher, but also offers discipline-based explanations for why and how those experiences occurred. Those responsible for planning induction of new teachers will find much of value in this book, particularly for beginning to teach in urban settings.

Etheridge, Carol. P. In press, 1989. How teachers move from university learnings to school-based practices. *Action in Teacher Education* 11 (Spring). Describes a process through which beginning teachers' teaching behaviors become established, based on a synthesis of participant observations in two fifth year preparation/induction programs and ethnographic interviews with 31 consultants over a three-year period. Consultants were beginning secondary teachers who completed fifth year teacher preparation/induction programs and two years as certified teachers in rural, urban, or suburban school districts. This study provides useful and realistic insights into how the realities of the workplace often bring about undesirable strategic adjustments by beginning teachers.

Gehrke, Nathalie J. 1987. On helping the beginning teacher. In *The first year of teaching: Background papers and a proposal*, ed. Gary A. Griffin and Suzanne Millies, 105-13. Chicago: University of Illinois-Chicago. Examines the kinds of help for beginning teachers in light of what is known about beginnings. She discusses creation of a new helping community for teachers, a community that benefits both beginning teachers and experienced teachers as well. Gehrke's model is based on the notion that conditions must be created within schools that will assure sustained care for beginning teachers beyond those times when the public is concerned about teacher retention. She illustrates her helping community by using perspectives from sociology, anthropology, psychology, linguistics, and education. Gehrke cautions that the building of helping communities within each school should receive attention equal to, if not greater than, the development of large-scale technical assistance programs and training packages.

Griffin, Gary A. 1987. A state program for the initial year of teaching. In *The first year of teaching: Background papers and a proposal*, ed. Gary A. Griffin and Suzanne Millies, 129-37. Chicago: University of Illinois-Chicago. Sets forth a number of recommendations about how the state might act in relation to developing an Illinois Initial Year of Teaching Program. His recommendations attend to planning that must be engaged in as well as specific features of an initial year of teaching program that are believed to be essential. Griffin's capstone proposals are preceded by a brief presentation of the background against which any consideration of new teacher programs must be understood.

_____. 1985. Teacher induction: Research issues. *Journal of Teacher Education* 36 (1): 42-46. Asserts that although available research on beginning teachers and on induction programs has serious limitations, progress can be made by changing the research questions asked, and by improving the balance of qualitative and quantitative research methods employed to answer those questions. As have others, Griffin claims that there is little useful research available for use in induction programs. Great Britain and Australia, he notes, have studied induction more extensively, and can provide useful perspectives for researchers in the United States.

Griffin discusses the important distinction between "research that describes the experience of new teachers and research that gives attention to the influence of intentional interventions in the lives and work of new teachers" (p. 42). He notes that most research on new teachers has concentrated on describing problems in adjusting to their new role, but that few ameliorative programs are available. Griffin cautions against an overreliance on research on teaching as

116

a basis for designing induction programs, particularly those tied to certification of new teachers. He discusses several dilemmas associated with using research on teaching as the primary basis for induction programs. Griffin concludes this useful article by posing a series of questions for future research on teacher induction, and by presenting five pressing issues for teacher induction research.

Griffin, Gary A., and Millies, Suzanne, eds. 1987. *The first years of teaching: Background papers and a proposal.* Chicago: University of Illinois–Chicago. Commissioned by the Illinois State Board of Education, this most useful collection of papers was one component of an exploration of the desirability of moving ahead with an Illinois Initial Year of Teaching Program. Written by recognized national experts in their respective fields, the topics of the papers are ones that have been shown in other states and regions to be of importance in planning, implementing, and assessing the impact of beginning teacher induction programs. This collection of papers, in combination with the reports of current teacher induction practices provided in the ATE National Commission (see Brooks 1987 above), provides an excellent starting point for understanding the current teacher induction knowledge base, issues, and practices.

Hall, Gene. 1982. Induction: The missing link. *Journal of Teacher Education* 33 (3): 53-55. Notes the gap between higher education and the local school district responsibility for teacher induction, and calls for a career-long view of teacher development that would include the transition from preservice to in-service. Hall observes that relatively little research has been done on the induction phase and that "almost no research has focused on strategies to assist teachers during this time" (p. 52). Like Griffin, Hall recognizes that educators in Great Britain and Australia have induction programs in place, and have conducted systematic studies of induction. He goes on to suggest that socialization research from industrial and organizational theory can provide useful starting points for educators' study of teacher socialization. He concludes by offering an extensive list of research questions generated by participants in an invited AERA Division C forum on induction. Hall suggests five topics as starting points for induction research: (a) the phenomena of induction, (b) induction teacher education programs, (c) selection, (d) retention, and (e) linkage.

Hawk, Parmalee. 1984. *Making a difference: Reflections and thoughts of first year teachers.* Greenville, NC: School of Education, East Carolina University. Based on over one hundred hours of tape-recorded interviews with twenty-eight first-year teachers employed in public school systems in rural northeastern North Carolina, this publication captures the thoughts and experiences of these teachers in an enlightening and interesting manner. Hawk writes that *Making a Difference* "was not written to report hard empirical data from which highly reliable inferences or generalizations can be made. Rather it was written to capture some of the impressions of . . . beginning teachers" (p. ii). Drawing heavily on quotes from the first-year teachers, the book is organized in seven chapters around such themes as reasons for choosing to teach, facing the realities of paperwork and continuous responsibility; planning; instruction; evaluation; discipline and relations with parents and principals.

Hawk, Parmalee, and Robards, Shirley. 1987. Statewide teacher induction programs. In *Teacher induction: A new beginning*, ed. Douglas M. Brooks, 33–44. Reston, VA: Association of Teacher Educators. Reports results of a survey of the status of statewide teacher induction programs. Reporting responses from 50 states, they discuss components of implemented statewide teacher induction programs, as well as components of statewide programs in the pilot stage of implementation. A useful name/address list of contacts for each state is included. An excellent and current overview of induction activity at the state level.

Hegler, Kay, and Dudley, Richard. 1987. Beginning teacher induction: A progress report. *Journal of Teacher Education* 38 (January-February): 53-56. Documents implementation of an induction program as one component in teacher education reform. Hegler and Dudley identify the general purposes of induction programs and describe how this specific program addresses these purposes. Explains the roles of the college supervisor and of the support teacher. Describes the program's unique features, and its strengths and weaknesses. The authors recommend implementation of college-based induction programs and present suggestions for program development and additional research.

Hitz, Randy, and Roper, Susan. 1986. The teacher's first year: Implications for teacher educators. *Action in Teacher Education* 8 (Fall): 65-71. Assigns the general needs of beginning teachers into four categories based on a conceptual analysis of related professional literature. The authors maintain that beginning teachers need (a) to learn to work with other adults: parents, administrators, and aides; (b) to learn to work effectively with other teachers; (c) to acquire a more realistic view of the work of teaching; and (d) to be provided a more useful and comprehensive theoretical framework on which to base initial professional development.

Howey, Kenneth, and Bents, Richard, eds. 1979. *Toward meeting the needs of the beginning teacher: Initial training/induction/inservice.* Minneapolis: Midwest Teacher Corps Network and University of Minnesota/St. Paul Schools Teacher Corps Project. Addresses the needs and issues concerning beginning teachers; reviews lessons learned from past induction efforts; offers conceptual, theoretical and operational models for teacher induction; and presents challenges, issues, and research questions for the future. This unified collection of nine papers provides an historical overview of some of the more common efforts that have been employed to help beginning teachers; discusses problems facing beginning teachers; outlines the need for a comprehensive set of guidelines for policy makers; reviews issues associated with internship programs; reinforces the need for cooperation among public school personnel, higher education, state legislatures, boards of education and certification officers; explores needed research and research issues related to the beginning years of teaching; outlines an operational model for support of beginning teachers from the perspective of a school administrator; expresses concern about the amount of time and type of initial preparation, the overemphasis on "hands on" activity, and the tendency of teacher selection and socialization to foster a conservative outlook and resistance to change in teachers; provides a model for the induction of beginning teachers based on developmental theory; and concludes with a general framework for induction and continuing teacher education that provides a means of considering each of the various decisions faced in planning a comprehensive and unified induction program.

Howey, Kenneth R., and Zimpher, Nancy. 1987. The role of higher education in the initial year of teaching programs. In *The first year of teaching: Background papers and a proposal*, ed. Gary A. Griffin and Suzanne Millies, 35-64. Chicago: University of Illinois-Chicago. Examines appropriate roles for those in institutions of higher education (IHE) in terms of enabling beginning teachers in their initial years of teaching. Howey and Zimpher begin by emphasizing that major changes in funding arrangements and cooperative working relationships are necessary. Their comprehensive paper is based on the assumptions that (a) new teachers first learn much essential knowledge about teaching on the job rather than in preservice preparation programs; (b) induction support and opportunities for learning are necessities rather than niceties for many beginning teachers; (c) initial education of teachers is a joint responsibility of IHEs and K-12 schools, and extends well into the beginning years of teaching; and (d) intensive intervention to correct induction problems is long overdue. They discuss in detail eight specific activities in which IHEs should engage collaboratively with those in K-12 schools in order to contribute to improved assistance to beginning teachers.

Huling-Austin, Leslie. In press. Teacher induction and internships. In *Handbook of research on teacher education*. ed. W. Robert Houston. New York: Macmillan and Association of Teacher Educators. Defines and establishes teacher induction in relation to career-long teacher education. In her comprehensive examination of current developments in the field of teacher induction and internships, Huling-Austin reviews state and national induction policy; describes and discusses various sponsors/sources of induction programs; discusses various common components of induction programs and internships, and explores potential conceptual paradigms useful for structuring teacher induction programs. Her consideration of research on teacher induction includes studies of needs and concerns of beginning teachers; research on induction programs, practices, and internships; and closely examines research on the influence of context on beginning teachers. Huling-Austin summarizes areas of consensus about teacher induction and then reviews unresolved issues. This well-organized chapter concludes with discussion of needed next steps in the areas of policy, practice, and research. This chapter is timely and will be of assistance to those developing induction programs and conducting research in this important area.

_____. 1987. Teacher induction. In *Teacher induction: A new beginning*, ed. Douglas M. Brooks, 3-24. Reston, VA: Association of Teacher Educators.

119

Summarizes progress on teacher induction that has been made in the United States during the past decade and provides a knowledge-based context for understanding teacher induction programs and activities. She considers several critical professional issues that must be addressed if teacher induction programs are to accomplish their goals, and concludes with a discussion of needed next steps and recommendations for future directions in teacher induction research practice.

_____. ed, 1986. *Induction directory*. Washington, DC: Association of Teacher Educators. Contains brief descriptions of over one hundred teacher induction programs on-going in school systems and higher education institutions across the United States. Initially a project of the Model Teacher Induction Program (MTIP) established by the Research and Development Center for Teacher Education at the University of Texas at Austin, the Association of Teacher Educators National Commission on the Induction Process has updated the *Induction Directory* based on information obtained from school systems, professional organizations, and institutions of higher education. Each directory entry contains a contact name, address, and a brief description of the program.

Ishler, Peggy, and Kester, Ralph. 1987. Professional organizations and teacher induction: Initiatives and positions. In *Teacher Induction: A new beginning*, ed. Douglas M. Brooks, 61-68. Reston, VA: Association of Teacher Educators. Discusses teacher induction initiatives and positions of professional organizations. Within a meaningful historical context, the authors summarize professional organizations' recommendations on nine critical issues in teacher induction. A useful overview of the professional perspective on beginning teacher induction.

Johnston, John M. 1985. Teacher induction: Problems, roles and guidelines. In *Career-long teacher education*, ed. Peter J. Burke and Robert G. Heideman, 194-222. Springfield, IL: Charles C Thomas. Proposes goals to be accomplished by a comprehensive induction program and then reviews problems of beginning teachers as a context for planning induction programs. Johnston's review of the professional needs and problems of beginning teachers includes topics of: (a) pupil instruction and classroom management; (b) relations with other teachers, administrators, parents, and community; (c) reality/culture shock; and (d) isolation, anxiety, and self-doubt. He also considers the personal needs and problems of beginning teachers. He discusses problems related to clarity of purpose for induction programs, problems of tradition, and problems of financing. Johnston presents guidelines for designing teacher induction programs, and discusses the need for cooperation among the three groups sharing major responsibility for teacher induction. Roles and contributions from the local school level, university and teacher education programs, and state or intermediate state agencies are presented and discussed. This essay concludes with a call for individualized and personalized teacher induction programs.

Johnston, John M., and Kay, Richard. 1987. The role of institutions of higher education in professional teacher induction. In *Teacher induction: A new beginning*, ed. Douglas M. Brooks, 45-60. Reston, VA: Association of Teacher Educators. Reports survey results from 300 responding teacher education institutions who were members of the American Association of Colleges of Teacher Education. Johnston and Kay consider roles to be played by institutions of higher education (IHE) in the professional induction of beginning teachers. Five goals of teacher induction programs are presented as a context for IHE participation in teacher induction. Selected factors affecting optimal IHE involvement are discussed. The survey results are reported and discussed and suggestions for IHE involvement in beginning teacher induction are presented.

Jordell, Karl. 1987. Structural and personal influences in the socialization of beginning teachers. *Teaching and Teacher Education* 3 (3): 165-77. Discusses the relative importance of different forms of influence on the beginning teacher and teachers at large. The personal and structural influences of the classroom, the institution, the society and the teachers' own recollections of experiences as pupils in schools and students in teacher education are explored. Jordell's useful conceptual analysis suggests that the structural influences at the classroom level are of primary importance, while experiences as a pupil and as a teacher education student probably have more limited impact.

Kester, Ralph, and Marockie, Mary. 1987. Local induction programs. In *Teacher induction: A new beginning*, ed. Douglas M. Brooks, 25-32. Reston, VA: Association of Teacher Educators. Reports the results of the Association of Teacher Educators National Commission on the Induction Process survey of beginning teacher programs in 1,100 local school systems in 17 states. Information is provided regarding teacher induction strategies employed, amount of time spent for induction, the intent or purpose of induction programs, evaluation of induction programs, issues of compensation for time spent in induction, voluntary or mandatory participation in induction activities, and concludes with a report of what factors facilitate successful induction programs.

Lasley, Thomas, ed. 1986. Teacher induction: Programs and research. *Journal of Teacher Education* 37 (1). Contains a powerful and useful thematic collection of articles on programs and research in teacher induction. Leslie Huling-Austin presents four goals for teacher induction programs, as well as reasonable and unreasonable expectations for such programs. This article represents an excellent starting point for those who are designing induction programs for beginning teachers. Cleta Galvez-Hjornevik presents a review of some of the most important, recent research on mentoring among teachers. She identifies the salient characteristics of successful mentor-protege relationships. She also argues that knowledge of induction from other disciplines and fields be incorporated into planning teacher induction programs. Sandra Fox and Ted Singletary propose a set of goals for teacher induction programs and discuss components for induction programs. James Hoffman and his colleagues from the University of Texas Research and Development Center for Teacher Education report findings from a large-scale investigation of two state-mandated beginning teacher programs. The research was designed to document how beginning teacher programs af-

121

fect the transition from student of teaching to regular classroom teacher. Gail Huffman and Sarah Leak report their study of 108 new teachers' reactions to a mentoring support program. Of particular value are their research-based recommendations for design and conduct of beginning teacher mentor programs. Sandra Odell reports a study of the needs of both first-year teachers and "new to the system" teachers participating in a teacher inducation program. Of particular interest is her finding that experienced teachers who are new to a school system do not have remarkably different needs from those of first-year teachers. Leonard Varah and his colleagues describe the University of Wisconsin-Whitewater Teacher Induction Program, and present results of a program evaluation study. Dorothy Stewart presents a useful annotation of selected articles and documents indexed in the ERIC system. Of particular interest, Stewart notes that "teacher orientation" is the ERIC descriptor used for the concept of teacher induction, a term so new that it is not yet included in the current *ERIC Thesaurus*. She further notes that "beginning teacher induction" is being developed as a descriptor, and is currently in use as an identifier. The collection of teacher induction articles in this issue of *JTE* concludes with reaction to the articles from Marilyn Rauth, Executive Director of the Educational Issues Department, American Federation of Teachers; and G. Robert Bowers, Assistant Superintendent of Public Instruction, State of Ohio.

Maryland State Department of Education & Research for Better Schools, Inc. 1987. *Perspective on teacher induction: A review of the literature and promising program models.* Baltimore: Author. Intended for educational leaders, this three-section monograph presents information and perspectives regarding support given to beginning teachers. The first section reviews a variety of perspectives on the purposes that teacher induction programs can serve. Among the perspectives addressed are those based on studies of beginning teachers' perceived needs, effective teaching research, teacher socialization, stages of concern, and adult development. The second section describes the types of support provided by different teacher induction programs, including specific descriptions of nine programs. The final section summarizes suggestions found in the literature regarding the design of teacher induction programs.

McDonald, Frederick J., and Elias, Pat. 1982. *The transition into teaching: The problems of beginning teachers and programs to solve them. Summary report.* Berkeley, CA: Educational Testing Service. Reports a study "undertaken to determine with greater precision what is known about the problems of beginning teachers, and to describe as accurately and completely as possible the means which have been used to anticipate, prevent, resolve or ameliorate these problems" (p. 3). McDonald and Elias go on to present a diversified survey of two kinds of programs: (1) internship programs, and (2) induction programs (". . . programs in which the beginning teacher participates when they are first employed full time with full teaching responsibility assigned to them" [p. 3]). As McDonald and Elias offer an analysis of characteristics of existing programs, they chronicle the problems of beginning teachers, discuss existing internship and induction programs, and conclude with recommended studies of the beginning teacher. In the introduction, however, they point out that after completing the study "We are left with a conundrum. We do not know whether to improve the quality of teacher preparation or whether some special form of assistance is required during the transition into teaching, or whether radically new forms of teacher preparation should be tried" (p. 2).

Odell, Sandra. 1987. Teacher induction: Rationale and issues. In *Teacher induction: A new beginning*, ed. Douglas M. Brooks, 69-80. Reston, VA: Association of Teacher Educators. Considers rationale and issues for teacher induction. She explores beginning teacher concerns, stages of teacher development, administrative structural consideration, personnel considerations, and concludes with an excellent discussion of pedagogical considerations and issues.

Peterson, Ken. In press. Assistance and assessment of beginning teachers. In *Handbook for the evaluation of elementary and secondary school teachers*, ed. Jason Millman and Linda Darling-Hammond. Beverly Hills, CA: Sage. Explores the characteristics and the needs of beginning teachers, then discusses teacher induction assistance systems and presents components of comprehensive induction programs. Peterson includes consideration of evaluation for tenure and beyond. Throughout this chapter he is careful to consider issues related to formative and summative evaluation of beginning teachers, as well as the relationship between beginning teaching and career-long development. He argues that beginning teachers are in an unusual position with respect to evaluation: they expect it; they have not been socialized against it, or had bad experiences with it; and they need the feedback it provides. Peterson believes that educational systems should provide enhanced evaluation opportunities and procedures for beginning teachers.

Reynolds, M. C., ed. 1989. *Knowledge base for the beginning teacher.* Washington, DC: American Association of Colleges for Teacher Education. A major reference work for preservice/in-service teacher educators, this volume addresses one of the major problems in teacher education: the difference between "state of the art" and the "state of practice." This major effort by AACTE seeks to advance the state of teacher education by specifiying that body of knowledge that people should possess and ultimately be able to apply in order to begin teaching. Addresses general knowledge about teaching, pedagogy, the learner in context, subject-specific pedagogy, and the teacher as a professional.

Rosenholtz, Susan J. 1987. Workplace conditions of teacher quality and commitment: Implications for the design of teacher induction programs. In *The first year of teaching: Background papers and a proposal*, ed. Gary A. Griffin and Suzanne Millies, 15-34. Chicago: University of Illinois-Chicago. Explores the alarming trend for teachers with the potential for making the greatest academic contributions to schools to be the most likely to leave teaching early in their careers. In this important paper, Rosenholtz considers several school conditions required for teachers' productive commitment to schools. She also explores the discouraging picture of the consequences where these workplace conditions fail to be met. Inconsiderable detail, she outlines how schools can be structured to enhance teachers' learning opportunities and their sense of teaching efficacy, with particular emphasis on beginning teachers. Finally, she details ten specific policy implications for the design of teacher induction programs.

Rossetto, Celeste R., and Grosenick, Judith K. 1987. Effects of collaborative teacher education: Follow-up of graduates of a teacher induction program. *Journal of Teacher Education* 38 (March-April): 50-52. Investigates perceptions of graduates in a program that combines on-the-job training with induction activities. Program graduates from the past 13 years were surveyed regarding the training they received. Results indicate that most graduates remained in teaching, and rated program objectives as having been attained.

Ryan, Kevin. 1986. *The induction of new teachers.* Fastback #237. Bloomington, IN: Phi Delta Kappa Educational Foundation. Details six of the most common problems that face first-year teachers: the shock of the familiar, students, parents, administrators, fellow teachers, and instruction itself. In this well-written booklet, Ryan eloquently describes how assistance with these problems can come from beginning teachers themselves, school districts, and teacher training institutions.

Ryan, Kevin; Newman, Katherine K.; Mager, Gerald; Applegate, Jane; Lasley, Thomas; Flora, V. Randall; and Johnston, John M. 1980. *Biting the apple: Accounts of first year teachers.* New York: Longman. Provides a detailed exploration of the mismatch between beginning teacher expectations and on-the-job realities, based on an intensive ethnographic study of eighteen first-year teachers. Most of the book consists of accounts of the first-year teaching experiences of twelve of the study's eighteen participants. Using an inside voices–outside eyes perspective, these accounts combine the experiences of the first-year teachers with the perspective of the researchers who intensively studied them during their first year. Based on hundreds of hours of interviews, observations, informal conversation, questionnaires, and contacts with other inhabitants of the first-year teachers' world, the researchers' field notes have been woven into accounts that document the successes and failures of first-year teachers in a variety of settings. The twelve accounts in *Biting the Apple* are fertile sources of information about beginning teachers' lives both inside and outside the classroom, and as such provide a valuable perspective for those seeking to understand the needs of new teachers in the induction phase of teacher career development.

Schlechty, Phillip. 1985. A framework for evaluating induction into teaching. *Journal of Teacher Education* 36 (1): 37-41. Identifies the indicators and characteristics of effective induction systems. In this very useful article, Schlechty writes ''an effective induction system is a system that creates conditions in which new members to the . . . occupation so internalize the norms peculiar to the

124

group that they conform to these norms" (p. 37). Schlechty discusses norms in relation to the induction of professionals, and then identifies three indicators of effective induction systems: (a) the way in which the norms are distributed throughout the group; (b) the patterns of conformity that develop around the norms; and (c) the patterns of deviation from the norms. The bulk of the article is devoted to discussion of eight characteristics of effective induction systems. He then describes efforts within the Charlotte-Mecklenburg Schools' Career Development Program to incorporate these characteristics. Schlechty concludes with an analysis of the fundamental changes needed in the way teacher education is conceptualized by school personnel.

Shulman, J. H., and Colbert, J. A., eds. 1988. *The intern teacher casebook.* Far West Laboratory for Educational Research and Development, ERIC Clearinghouse on Educational Management, and ERIC Clearinghouse on Teacher Education. The second in a series of Close-to-the Classroom Casebooks developed collaboratively by researchers, staff developers, and teacher trainees, this volume is a part of the Effective Support for Beginning Teachers Program, and contains cases on selected first-year experiences, written by the trainees themselves. The problems described are similar to those that any novice might face during the first year of teaching in a school located in a large metropolitan area. All the narratives (vignettes) included in this book are representative of a larger class of experiences common to the first year of teaching. Includes cases of beginning teachers dealing with classroom events that are problematic either in their conception or their implementation; interactions with students who are disruptive or refuse to work; and relationships with mentor teachers or other experienced teachers who attempt to help. Each case contains four parts: the academic background and previous experience of the trainee; a description of the classroom, school, and students; a narration of a classroom event or interaction; and some reflective thoughts about the account by experienced teachers or scholars.

———. 1987. *The mentor teacher casebook.* Far West Laboratory for Educational Research and Development, ERIC Clearinghouse on Educational Management, and ERIC Clearinghouse on Teacher Education. The first in a series of Close-to-the Classroom Casebooks, this volume was developed with researchers and mentor teachers in a large metropolitan school district. This casebook provides illustrative vignettes, written by the mentor teachers, of their work with first-year teachers. The cases presented describe the circumstances of each event, its consequences, and the ongoing thoughts and feelings of the participants. The case narratives are grouped by issues and are accompanied by brief analytical commentaries by the editors. The cases included in this book focus on the process of mentoring: establishing the working relationship, individual consultation, observing and coaching, and modeling; relationship between mentors and principals; and issues affecting the life of a mentor: novice teachers with novice mentors, rewards, frustrations, relations with others, and friendships with other teachers.

Smith, David C., and Wilson, Garfield W. 1986. The Florida Beginning Teacher Program. In *The dynamics of change in teacher education. Volume I: Background papers for the National Commission for Excellence in Teacher Education*, ed. Thomas J. Lasley, 127-41. Washington, DC: American Association of Colleges for Teacher Education. Describes how a comprehensive and integrated system of support, training, and evaluation is designed to accomplish two central purposes: the improvement of beginning teachers and the documentation of their successful performance. The legislative background, development of the model, and implementation of the program is described. The outcomes yielded by the Florida Beginning Teacher Program are described.

Veenman, S. 1984. Perceived problems of beginning teachers. *Review of Educational Research* 54 (2): 143-78. Reviews and analyzes research on the perceived problems of beginning teachers in the most recent and most comprehensive treatment of this much publicized topic. Veenman's abstract of this paper is presented below.

Perceived problems of beginning teachers in their first year of teaching are reviewed. Studies from different countries are included. Issues such as the reality shock and changes in behaviors and attitudes are considered also. The eight problems perceived most often are classroom discipline, motivating students, dealing with individual differences, assessing students' work, relationships with parents, organization of class work, insufficient and/or inadequate teaching materials and supplies, and dealing with problems of individual students. There is a great correspondence between the problems of elementary and secondary beginning teachers. Issues such as person-specific and situation-specific differences, views of the principals, problems of experienced teachers, and job satisfactions of beginning teachers are discussed also. Three frameworks of teacher development are presented which provide conceptualizations of individual differences among beginning teachers. Finally, forms of planned support for beginning teachers are noted. Research using an interactionist model for the explanation of behavior is needed. (p. 143)

Ward, Beatrice. 1987. State and district structures to support initial year of teaching programs. In *The first year of teaching: Background papers and a proposal*, ed. Gary A. Griffin and Suzanne Millies, 1-14. Chicago: University of Illinois-Chicago. Explores state and district structures to support initial year of teacher programs. Ward considers several structures that have promise for supporting development and installation of initial year of teaching programs. Her perspective is shaped by research on effective teaching, effective teacher training, school-based staff development, and knowledge production and utilization in education. She recommends specific action in three areas: (a) provision of training and services for novice teachers, (b) interinstitutional arrangements that foster collaborative design and implementation of training and support services, and (c) standards to guide design and implementation of initial year of teaching programs. Six structures are proposed and discussed that support action in these three areas: (a) mentor teachers, (b) teacher development schools, (c) school district-university collaboratives, (d) a center for quality teaching, (e) initial years of teaching program standards, and (f) teacher advancement standards.

Yinger, Robert J. 1987. Learning the language of practice: Implications for beginning year of teaching programs. In *The first year of teaching: Background papers and a proposal*, ed. Gary A. Griffin and Suzanne Millies, 65-89. Chicago: University of Illinois-Chicago. Argues persuasively that a major task confronting the beginning teacher is a learning to think and behave in ways appropriate to the demands of teaching, or what he refers to as "learning the language of practice" (p. 65). Yinger further argues that beginning teachers cannot learn this language of practice until they actually engage in teaching. Yinger presents a comprehensive argument by examining two sets of questions: (a) How might the knowledge and skill of the experienced practitioner best be described? and (b) How do teachers learn to teach? Using a study of beginning teachers learning to teach in order to illustrate some of the issues involved in acquiring a language of practice, he proposes ideas for describing the language of practice of teachers.

Zaharias, Jane Ann, and Frew, Thomas W. 1987. Teacher induction: An analysis of one successful program. *Action in Teacher Education* 9 (Spring): 49-55. Describes an induction program designed by one university to provide a nonthreatening forum wherein beginning teachers could discuss common concerns and seek the advice and assistance of master teachers. Program goals are stated, program implementation details related to staffing, recruitment, and location and scheduling are described. Program structure and content, and program outcomes are reported.

Zeichner, Kenneth. 1983. Individual and institutional factors related to the socialization of teachers. In *First years of teaching: What are the pertinent issues?* ed. Gary Griffin and H. Hukill. Austin, TX: Research and Development Center for Teacher Education. ERIC Document Reproduction Service No. 240 109. Argues that the induction process is more complex, contradictory and context specific than has been commonly thought. In this comprehensive essay, one of four papers published in the proceedings from a national working conference on teacher induction, Zeichner first considers who and what appear to influence the socialization of beginning teachers. Next, he examines how beginning teachers affect the system. Third, he addresses the thorny issue of generalization in relation to studies of beginning teacher socialization. Finally, he discusses the need for an administrative response to the presence of beginning teachers. Ken Zeichner is a teacher educator who has studied and published widely about the socialization of beginning teachers. This thoughtful essay is an excellent introduction to his scholarship, and includes a rich reference list on teacher socialization and induction.

THE CONTRIBUTORS

Victoria L. Bernhardt is Director, Institute for Advanced Studies in Education, California State University, Chico.

Maurice C. Erly is Coordinating Supervisor of Staff Development, Prince George's County Public Schools, Upper Marlboro, Maryland.

Carol P. Etheridge is Assistant Professor, Center of Excellence in Teacher Education, Memphis State University, Tennessee.

James D. Greenberg is Director, Office of Laboratory Experiences, College of Education, University of Maryland, College Park.

Marvin A. Henry is Chairperson, Department of Secondary Education, Indiana State University, Terre Haute.

Leslie Huling-Austin is Director of the LBJ Institute for the Improvement of Teaching and Learning and Associate Professor in the School of Education, Southwest Texas State University in San Marcos, Texas.

John M. Johnston is Associate Professor, Department of Curriculum and Instruction, Memphis State University, Tennessee.

Alvah M. Kilgore is Professor, Center for Curriculum and Instruction, University of Nebraska, Lincoln.

Julie A. Kozisek is Assistant Professor, Doane College, Crete, Nebraska.

Sandra J. Odell is Director, Teacher Induction, and Associate Professor, Department of Curriculum and Instruction in Multicultural Teacher Education, The University of New Mexico, Albuquerque.

Linda Parker is Associate Director, CESA 5, Portage, Wisconsin.

Judy Reinhartz is Assistant Director for the Center of Professional Teacher Education, Editor of *Centering Teacher Education*, and Professor at the University of Texas, Arlington.

Warren S. Theune is Assistant Dean (retired) at the University of Wisconsin-Whitewater.

Leonard J. Varah is former Coordinator, Teacher Induction Program, the University of Wisconsin-Whitewater.

Louise Bay Waters is University Director, Oakland-California State University, Hayward, New Teacher Support Program, and Associate Professor of Teacher Education at Hayward.